MW00795255

NEWMAN'S
VISIONARY
GEORGIC

PETER LANG
New York • Washington, D.C./Baltimore • Bern
Frankfurt am Main • Berlin • Brussels • Vienna • Oxford

Victor J. Lams

NEWMAN'S VISIONARY GEORGIC

A Reading of
Parochial Sermons

BX
5133
.N4
P3536
2006

PETER LANG
New York • Washington, D.C./Baltimore • Bern
Frankfurt am Main • Berlin • Brussels • Vienna • Oxford

Library of Congress Cataloging-in-Publication Data

Lams, Victor J.
Newman's visionary georgic: a reading of Parochial sermons /
Victor J. Lams.
p. cm.
Includes bibliographical references (p.   ) and index.
1. Newman, John Henry, 1801–1890. Parochial sermons.
2. Church of England—Sermons—History and criticism.
3. Sermons, English—19th century—
History and criticism. I. Title.
BX5133.N4P3536   251.0092—dc22   2006004965
ISBN 0-8204-6377-9

Bibliographic information published by **Die Deutsche Bibliothek**.
Die Deutsche Bibliothek lists this publication in the "Deutsche
Nationalbibliografie"; detailed bibliographic data is available
on the Internet at http://dnb.ddb.de/.

The paper in this book meets the guidelines for permanence and durability
of the Committee on Production Guidelines for Book Longevity
of the Council of Library Resources.

© 2006 Peter Lang Publishing, Inc., New York
29 Broadway, New York, NY 10006
www.peterlang.com

All rights reserved.
Reprint or reproduction, even partially, in all forms such as microfilm,
xerography, microfiche, microcard, and offset strictly prohibited.

Printed in Germany

To
SUSAN DEBLOUW LAMS
AND
CECELIA FARLEY WRIGHT

Contents

INTRODUCTION
Visionary Georgics

In *Newman's Anglican Georgic* (2004) I presented the evidence that *Parochial Sermons* should be considered a literary work, a georgic, and suggested in passing that it is Newman's enduring literary achievement. That suggestion may strike one as fatuous because the current definition of literature excludes sermons. But like ice ages, which last for a long while yet eventually recede, definitions of literature expand and contract over time. Leaving time to pass judgment upon that work's claim to literary greatness, this book undertakes a more modest task. It provides a careful reading of *Parochial Sermons* that examines Newman's practice as a sermonist intent upon enriching his readers' understanding of Christian doctrine and commitment to practical devotion, and as an architect who crafts well-designed individual volumes into a rhetorically coherent sequential structure. Such a reading requires that this collection of sermons be placed in the context of Newman's century by relating it to the intellectual history of post-Reformation Christianity. That necessary contextualizing is presented in the Prologue following this Introduction, whose more immediate purpose is to define the visionary georgic and relate *Parochial Sermons* to the other exemplars of that distinctive subset of the genre.

The georgic genre is characterized by its giving moral reflections on the conditions of human life and advice on the extent and the means by which a person can improve his situation. The dictionary definition of a georgic tells us that it is a poem about farming and rural life. But the reality is that the farmer in classical georgic represents Everyman, and the problems to be overcome in raising crops and livestock despite inclement weather, plant and animal diseases and the incremental depredations of mice and birds provides the metaphor that represents the difficulties of successful living, whatever one's occupation be. Now the visionary georgic is a subset of the genre characterized by its considerable length and correspondingly greater detail, and above all by its preoccupation with a single message, a central truth presented as indispensable to the reader's spiritual welfare. *Works and Days* is not a visionary georgic by this definition because, while Hesiod provides a single message (work hard, be honest and avoid evil), his georgic is too short, its contents too diffuse to meet the definition I am here advancing. Nor is Virgil's *Georgics* visionary in the sense proposed, for although sufficiently long and admirably constructed, it advances no foundational truth which the reader is counselled to embrace. To the contrary, it is harrassed by philosophical and theological questions which the agricultural metaphor is sufficient to activate, but questions never resolved by adequate answers. Virgil's provisional possibilities held in balance against one another are very unlike the enthusiastic embrace of a central existential truth which characterizes the visionary georgicist.

If Hesiod and Virgil did not write visionary georgics, who did? Lucretius, Wordsworth and Newman wrote them, and their example shows that the truth which such a georgic inculcates need not be original, unique and unprecedented, but it must be single-mindedly concentrated on that truth. It must be driven by personal conviction, along with the writer's powerful interpretation of human destiny in light of that conviction. Take Lucretius for example. The core of his visionary georgic is that all of reality consists of atoms that are constantly in motion and occasionally swerve and that religion is therefore fraudulent because the human soul is material and dies along with the body. Such is the saving truth he is determined to drive home on Memmius—not the historical Roman so named, but the Memmius of the poem, the reader internal to the poem, or what Diskin Clay calls "the creature of *De rerum natura*," the perplexed person who is unsettled by his "feelings of constraint and inhibition" about the gods (221), whose conversion to Epicurean wisdom is this author's constant preoccupation. Did Lucretius show any interest in the scientific advancements going on in the Roman think tanks of his day? Not at all. As David Sedley shows, he ignored "the highly charged philosophical atmosphere" of his own country and century because his inspiration "comes from the unmediated scriptures of the philosopher he reveres . . . Like any fundamentalist, he does not expect the numerous contributions made since the composition of his scriptures . . . to have added anything worth taking into account." It is irrelevant to Lucretius whether intelligence resides in the stomach or the brain; what concerns him is that Epicurus was "a god who eclipsed the traditional Olympian deities in the importance of his benefactions to mankind" (65, 71–2), chief among them being his program for overcoming trepidations about disasters in life and fear of punishment after death through an enabling realization that death is the end of all, the fruit of that realization being peace.

As H. N. Fairchild points out, "'the predicament of modern man' has been creeping up on us for a long while—intermittently since Lucretius and almost continuously since the sixteenth century" (V, 395). That observation provides a segue to Wordsworth, the inheritor and champion of Protestantism's gradual rejection of Christian doctrine. Wordsworth feels confident that his vocation is to become Milton's successor, the visionary whose destiny is to carry forward the earlier seer's theological position and square it with the contemporary intellectual milieu. To do so he dismisses supernatural religion, not by repudiating it, but by naturalizing it, conceiving of it as originating not in God's revelation but in human imagination. He advances the revolution in western thought (Prologue) which established the trajectory he would travel. Two factors contributed to his success. First, Wordsworth had no personal commitment to supernatural religion, and second, he had drunk deeply in physico-theology through his close study of eighteenth-century poetry. R. D. Havens believes that "any study of Wordsworth's religion" must inevitably conclude that his religious beliefs cannot be formulated because he himself was unclear about them. "Today he was an orthodox Anglican; tomorrow he felt there were spirits in the woods and lonely places; then again he was conscious of an infinite force pervading all things" (197). To be sure, Wordsworth felt strong emotions about numinous realities, but these were amorphous, shifting, untethered to anything stable or definite. Thus, for example, when in Book I of *The Prelude* he bursts into fervent praise of what he addresses as "Wisdom and Spirit of the Universe!/ Thou Soul that art the eternity of thought,/ That giv'st to forms and images a breath/ And everlasting Motion" (401–4), it is impossible to determine precisely who or what he is addressing, though it is evident that he has embarked upon a grand O *altitudo*.

The second enabling factor in Wordsworth's progress as a Romantic visionary was his indebtedness to the line of Protestant thought which had been progressively emerging in English poetry before him. Based upon his close study of that poetry, Fairchild informs us that "Wordsworth could have derived every element of his nature-religion from the eighteenth-century poets whom he is known to have read with such close attention," beginning with Akenside, Beattie, Blake, Burns, Chatterton and Collins and proceeding through the alphabet down to Thomson's *Seasons*. For Akenside and Wordsworth alike, "poetic imagination is the reflection of divine creativeness in the human soul." For both men, "poetry is religion, and religion is poetry" (Fairchild, III, 186–88). In the conventional assumptions of the time, it was simply axiomatic that the universe was a harmony of benevolence, that external nature was not only morally beneficial but in some sense numinous, that man's native impulses possessed a quality of goodness akin to the goodness of Nature and of Nature's God. III,164

Granting that Wordsworth got his religion from the poets he had studied, how had they contrived to turn Protestantism into an earth-bound belief system? M. H. Abrams identifies the process by which the forms of Christian doctrine were during this period radically reinterpreted: "Many of the most distinctive and recurrent elements in both the thought and literature of the age had their origin in theological concepts, images, and plot patterns." The general tendency of such adaptation was "to naturalize the supernatural and to humanize the divine" (*Natural Supernaturalism*, 65, 68). Abrams notices for example that in *The Prelude* God has "not quite dropped out, but He is mentioned only after the fact, and given nothing to do." He is "the purely formal reminder of His former self, because His traditional offices," such as creation and redemption, "have been preempted" by nature and the human imagination (*N.S.*, 89–90). Wordsworth makes it clear that in the exchange between the mind and nature that has been *The Prelude's* theme, "the protagonist had in fact been the power of his mind, so that what he has all along been narrating is the story of the birth, growth, disappearance, and resurrection of imagination." From the pertinent text which Abrams quotes in this regard (*N.S.*, 118), it becomes equally clear that Christ's descent from heaven to effect man's salvation has been obviated, replaced by an entirely human power which produces that result—a redemptive power that is figured as a flowing stream which, though it is now and then "lost sight of" by running underground, at last "rose once more/ With strength." John Bunyan would have been perplexed by the novel content here, but he would have recognized the plot structure.

As the co-existence of the whippet, the pomeranian and the spaniel enables us to better comprehend the nature of dogs, so does the existence of several visionary georgics allow us through comparison to better understand the nature of the visionary variation of the georgic genre. Thus, one can observe as a distinction between *De rerum natura* and *The Prelude*, that while Lucretius' argument is constantly punctuated by badgering, lapel-grabbing appeals to Memmius to accept and profit from Epicurus' message of freedom, the relationship between Wordsworth and his audience could best be described as recessive, the reader being represented at one remove by a shadowy stand-in, the "Friend" Wordsworth addresses, an alterego permitted enough separate existence to keep him from disappearing into the force-field of the author's creative imagination, who functions as an ear into which Wordsworth speaks to himself. Together, he and this diaphanous Friend are described as "joint labourers in the Work" of man's redemption, which is a "deliverance, surely yet to come" (XIV, 441–3) despite the disappointment of the French

Revolution's failure to achieve it. "Prophets of Nature," it is their mutual task to save "This Age," which has fallen back "to old idolatry," and all mankind, who "return to servitude" with disconcerting speed and agility. The redemptive agent will be love, because "what we have loved,/ Others will love, and we will teach them how" (XIV, 435–6, 446–9)). From these concluding comments it is clear that Wordsworth intends *The Prelude* to do precisely what georgics always do: reflect upon the human condition in the light of human possibility, with an eye to the existence, intervention, and benign or hostile intentions of the gods. Moreover, it has been made clear by the poem that all gods reside in the human breast, for Wordsworth informs us "Here must thou be, O Man!/ Power to thyself; no Helper hast thou here;/ Here keepest thou in singleness thy state." Thus, the all-important locus of salvation is to be found "In the recesses of thy nature, far/ From any reach of outward fellowship" (XIV, 209–11, 216–17). Not God alone, but the sacramental system and the Communion of Saints are thereby subsumed within the creative power of the individual.

Because visionary georgics concern themselves not with intermediate goals but ultimate aims, and since the number of plausible world hypotheses is small, the writers of such georgics tend to speak to one another across the ages, as do Lucretius and Wordsworth. When the latter apostrophizes "the Upholder of the tranquil soul,/ That tolerates the indignities of Time,/ And, from the centre of Eternity/ All finite motions overruling, lives/ In glory immutable" (III, 120–24), he runs afoul of Lucretius. For, as Diskin Clay observes, there is for Epicurus and Lucretius "no room for Physis—no divine and personified force that sustains and directs the world." Even as the concept of Mother Earth is being introduced in *De rerum natura* (2.600–60) she already is "the creature of mankind," an imaginary figure who is given wild beasts for her procession and a mural crown for her head, along with companions and attendants to offer her homage. Lucretius uses this element of Roman religion to exemplify "how men transform their real experience of the world into religion. It is a matter of *attribution*" (Clay, 87, 229). Attribution is Wordsworth's game, but Lucretius will have none of it, and differences such as these help us to better grasp the essential nature of visionary georgic.

As a last example of the interpretive value of setting different visionary georgics in comparison with each other, one observes the similarity between Lucretius and Newman in their reliance upon external authority for the truths which they offer their audiences, which sets them in the sharpest contrast against Wordsworth. In *The Mirror and the Lamp*, Abrams states that "As in the English Platonists, so in the romantic writers, the favorite analogy of the perceiving mind is that of a lamp projecting light" (60), and thus the lamp becomes the appropriate artifact to represent what he calls "expressive theories" of literature. In "pragmatic" theories, represented by the reflecting mirror which Hamlet would have the players hold up to human nature, the writer considers his literary creation "an instrument for getting something done." But for artists of the Lamp persuasion such as Wordsworth, "the poet's audience is reduced to a single member, consisting of the poet himself" (15, 25). Abrams notes that in Wordsworth's age "the poet has moved into the center of the critical system and taken over many of the prerogatives which had once been exercised by his readers, the nature of the world in which he found himself, and the inherited precepts and examples of his poetic art" (29). The relevant observation here is that the dismissal of inherited precept, accompanied by the individual's claim to discover truth by relying entirely on "the Candle of the Lord," was in Newman's day not limited to literature alone, nor had it originated therein. It was Protestantism's gift to literature, and the relation was vigorously reciprocal.

The Doctrinal Milieu
of *Parochial Sermons*

The six volumes of *Parochial Sermons* appeared during an interesting moment in the history of Protestantism—-one in which many who would have been Trinitarians at the Reformation had moved on to Unitarianism, that being the typical half-way house to rejecting Christianity altogether and embracing in its stead the secular scriptures of literature and the arts. Newman at that moment in history was engaged in a strong effort to defend the faith of the Apostles from what he perceived as corruptive trends. On the one hand he was writing tracts for the Oxford Movement in defense of the Anglican Church, while on the other he was composing and delivering weekly sermons for his Oxford parishoners. These two actions differ in that the tracts address a more public audience in a more polemical style, while the sermons speak to the inwardness of individual auditors with the intent of forming their character and guiding their thinking. Different though the tracts and sermons are in these respects, Dean Church in his history of the Oxford Movement testifies to the linkage between the two. He says "While men were reading and talking about the Tracts, they were hearing the sermons; and in the sermons they heard the living meaning, and reason, and bearing of the Tracts, their ethical affinities, their moral standard. The sermons created the moral atmosphere in which men judged the questions in debate" (130).

For us the crucial difference between Newman's sermons as weekly addresses with some bearing upon contemporaneous Tractarian themes and the volumes titled *Parochial Sermons* is this, that the questions of Newman's day have retreated into history with the *Tracts for the Times* which explored them, while *Parochial Sermons*, still in print, continues to articulate the living meaning, and reason, and bearing of what the Apostles taught. In these volumes one encounters the shrewd evaluative intellect of Newman, whose vision of what constitutes authentic Christianity is clear and whose pastoral advice is sound. I use the adjective "visionary" in the book's title in this sense, i.e., that Newman understood the contemporary religious situation and the stages through which English religion had metastasized since the Reformation, and furthermore, that he correctly anticipated its probable future. This facet of his visionary capacity is evident from his remarks, a quarter century following *Parochial Sermons'* publication, on the direction "fierce wilful human nature" was about to take, or to continue taking, a direction he saw shadowed forth in the current state of European society.

> The necessity of some form of religion for the interests of humanity, has been generally acknowledged: but where was the concrete representative of things invisible, which would have the force and the toughness necessary to be a breakwater against the deluge? Three centuries ago the establishment of religion, material, legal, and social, was generally adopted as the best expedient for the purpose, in those countries which separated from the Catholic Church; and for a long time it was successful; but now the crevices of those establishments are admitting the enemy. Thirty years ago, education was relied upon; ten years ago there was a hope that wars would cease forever, under the influence of commercial enterprise and the reign of the useful and fine arts; but will any one venture to say that there is any thing any where on this earth, which will afford a fulcrum for us, whereby to keep the earth from moving onwards? *Apologia* 232

Commonly it is the romantics whose views are valorized by the term visionary, while those whose views are contrary to theirs are called reactionaries. But that definition of the term reflects a vulgar prejudice which ought not to distract us here. What the romantic poet Yeats read about in the newspapers ("Mere anarchy is loosed upon the world,/ The blood-dimmed tide is loosed") Newman intuited in the events of his own century, which should demonstrate that romantic sensibilities have no monopoly on vision.

The best preparation for reading *Parochial Sermons* is to recollect the familiar course by which the intellectual assumptions of the western world were transformed, because that revolution in thinking provided the context in which Newman's Anglican Georgic was created. We will begin with "Prometheus Rising," the prologue which Harold Bloom added to his 1971 revision of *The Visionary Company: A Reading of English Romantic Poetry*. This commentary provides a useful perspective, for it is a brief retrospective picture of the trajectory of thought transformation from the standpoint of our own era. As Bloom points out, the religious background of all the English Romantic poets "was in the tradition of Protestant dissent, the kind of nonconformist vision that descended from the Left Wing of England's Puritan movement." The new trajectory onto which the Romantics put English poetry was not universally accepted but was opposed by those who found the change wrongheaded. Bloom observes that "the entire continuity of English poetry that T. S. Eliot and his followers attacked is a radical Protestant or displaced Protestant tradition," and thus one could justly say that the wars of religion did not end, they migrated into literature. Bloom continues, "It is no accident that the poets deprecated by the New Criticism were Puritans, or Protestant individualists, or men of that sort, breaking away from Christianity and attempting to formulate personal religions in their poetry" (xvii).

Bloom makes three points which are important to our reconstruction of *Parochial Sermons*' relationship to the intellectual revolution of the west. The first, as we have seen, is that the Romantics were attempting to formulate personal religions in their poetry. What laid the groundwork for that effort of religious invention? It was the gradual shift away from objective to subjective truth in areas other than physical science. Before the Romantics, the truths that were found in poetry were generally thought to be "dependent for their meanings" upon fields of knowledge such as theology, philosophy and history. What the Romantics did was to demote and dismiss those provinces of knowledge while at the same time making "the direct claim that poetry is prior to theology or moral philosophy, and by 'prior' they mean both more original and more intellectually powerful." This second of Bloom's points leads into the third, which is that the attribution of priority over traditional fields of knowledge amounts to "a metaphysic, a theory of history, and much more important than either of these," it is what all of the Romantics called "a vision, a way of seeing, and of living, a more human life" (xxiii-xiv). We can call this assertion the Romantic Vaunt, for it is the foundational principle of Romanticism. How it came to be triumphantly asserted, countermanding all claims to authority not originating in the subjectivity of the individual, we will now examine, because that radical shift in the source of authority is essential to seeing what Newman was up against.

Once Descartes had distinguished between two kinds of certainty, objective or external certainty which applies to mechanical causation, and subjective or internal certainty, the appeal to the inner tribunal of reason displaced external authority in religious matters. As Basil Willey puts it, "truth came to mean that which is vouched for by the 'inner light,' by 'Reason,' and the 'moral sense'" (83). A system that divides truth into two halves invites later thinkers to seize upon one and subordinate the other to it, as Hobbes did when, in Lucretian style, he reduced mind to an aspect of matter, a form of motion such that "the death of the body is the death of the man, since 'soul' for him simply means 'life.'" Although Hobbes did not publicly repudiate Christianity, he undermined it covertly, for "while leaving the outer shell of the orthodox structure to all appearances unaltered he is really at work rebuilding the interior with entirely new materials" (Willey, 117), as did others who followed him.

Lord Herbert of Cherbury and the Cambridge Platonists defined their own religious positions in reaction to Hobbes, yet in tacit cooperation with his undermining of orthodoxy. Hoping to find a reliable test of truth, Lord Herbert put his trust in the common religious notions generally held by everyone; these could be arrived at by either of two methods, "the study of comparative religion" or "the oracle within," the first of these being a superfluous task because inner certainty always trumps "laborious study" (131). Though Lord Herbert continues to use the word revelation, he means by it "some process of experience" (137) rather than something divinely revealed. The Cambridge Platonists, too, attempted to sidestep the tired vocabulary of religious controversy, and by doing so they also helped to undermine orthodoxy. "Mainly Puritan in affinity," the Platonists well illustrate what Willey describes as

> the tendency of advanced Protestant thought, after passing through its dogmatic post-Reformation phase, to reveal once again its original rationalizing temper, and to fall thus into line with the general movement of the [seventeenth] century. The Platonists are celebrated for their appeals to "Reason": Reason, which in the text which Whichcote especially never tires of quoting, is "the candle of the Lord," and to follow which, John Smith declares, is to follow God. 141

The Platonists opposed the implications of the Fall doctrine, insisting upon "the power of the individual to raise himself unceasingly towards perfection" (142), which is the position defended by the British monk Pelagius many centuries before. In this one can recognize "the Cartesian self-sufficiency, the Cartesian rejection of authority and reliance upon inward certitude" (145). In short, "that any truth could be 'given' by sheer force of supernatural authority, so that it must be believed without being understood," which is precisely Newman's position, "became less and less acceptable to most minds as the century proceeded" (Willey, 136). Given his purpose, which was to enable his Anglican parishoners to better reflect on their lives within the sessions of private thought, Newman in his sermons suppresses the voice of the polemicist who attacks the undermining of doctrinal truth which had been set going by the Cartesian revolution, a process which was spreading "like an infection of the air" in contemporary publications of Newman's century. Nevertheless, one could say that his sermons are informed by his trenchant reviews of books dangerous to revealed religion, the three most pertinent of these review essays being published in 1835, 1836 and 1841, dates which fall within the period when he was selecting and arranging the contents of *Parochial Sermons*.

The first of these review essays, "On the Introduction of Rationalistic Principles into Revealed Religion," begins by defining the corruption specified in the review's title before examining the rationalistic reductionism at work in Erskine's "Internal Evidence" and Abbott's "Corner Stone," both of these written by authors who considered themselves friends of Christianity and hoped to make it more palatable for contemporary people. Says Newman, "to rationalize in matters of Revelation is to make our reason the standard and measure of the doctrines revealed." This procedure is "the antagonist of Faith," which is "the acceptance of what our reason cannot reach, simply and absolutely upon testimony" (*Essays Critical and Historical*, Vol I, 31). With regard to the key distinction stemming from Descartes between objective and subjective truth and the subsequent identification of religion as consisting in "the reception of the latter," Newman redefines both of these varieties of truth and finds them equally applicable to religion. "By Objective Truth is meant the Religious System considered as existing in itself, external to this or that particular mind." On the other hand, "by Subjective, is meant that which each mind receives in particular, and considers to be such"—-that is, considers to be true, thereby in effect claiming veto power over what will be believed, what not. Newman expands the contrast between the two:

> To believe in objective truth is to throw ourselves forward upon that which we have but partially mastered or made subjective . . . [it is] to come before and bow before the import of such propositions, as if we were contemplating what is real and independent of human judgment. Such a belief, implicit, and symbolized as it is in the use of creeds, seems to the Rationalist superstitious and unmeaning, and he consequently confines Faith to the province of Subjective Truth, or to the reception of doctrine, as, and so far as, it is apprehended by the mind. 34–5

If in Newman's view rationalism is the chief enemy of religious truth in his day, its antidote is the constant voice of the Church over the centuries, a voice which he defends in "Apostolical Tradition" (1836), the occasion for this essay being a "small volume" which had just appeared, in which a clergyman and his Unitarian brother-in-law exchange disagreements about the Trinity. The commonly held error which guarantees that the two disputants will argue in circles without settling anything is the double supposition "that if we would ascertain the truths which Revelation has brought us, we have nothing else to do but to consult Scripture on the point, with the aid of our own private judgment, and that no doctrine is of importance which the Christian cannot find for himself in large letters there." Newman observes in this regard that "as Anglicans, we maintain that [Scripture] is not its own interpreter," that it has always had, "external to its readers and infallible," an interpreter derived from the Apostles, and that it is "this Tradition, and not Scripture itself," which constitutes "our immediate and practical authority for such high doctrines as these friends discuss" (*Essays Critical and Historical*, Vol I, 103).

Newman observes that his contemporary Blanco White, and before him Chillingworth and Locke, all of them more formidable adversaries than the two friends who argue at loggerheads in the "small volume" just published, believe "that Scripture has no authorized interpreter, and that dogmatic statements are no part of Revelation" (112–13). In this they are joined by "Dr. Hampden, to whose lot it has fallen to state objections to Catholic Truth in a more distinct shape than they have been found in the works of Churchmen for some time" (114). Writing of him in the year after Lord Melbourne appointed him Regius Professor of Divinity in Oxford, and thus "the head of the theological teaching of the university" (Church, 158), Newman says Dr. Hampden "assures us that the very idea of Tradition is a mistake, that there is no such thing as a succession of preaching and hearing," and that what is called Tradition teaches us "nothing more than Scripture," for tradition "is but the judgment of ecclesiastics exercised on Scripture" (116–17). Yet Newman insists that, "had Scripture never been written, Tradition would have existed still; it has an intrinsic, substantive authority, and a use collateral to Scripture." This is "the doctrine of genuine Anglicanism" (118–20). However, it was a doctrine which, as Newman's third important review essay suggests, was in subtle ways being repudiated by Churchmen in high places, men with more imposing educational credentials than theological wisdom.

One such was Henry Hart Milman, ten years Newman's senior, the third son of George III's physician, eventually appointed dean of St. Paul's——a person who had commanded attention by his performances in literature before turning his hand to church history and what we may call comparative theology, wherein Newman saw reductive rationalism at work. Milman was an Anglican priest who had had a "remarkably brilliant" Oxford career, was in 1821 elected as professor of poetry there, was in 1827 invited to deliver the Bampton lectures (an honor Dr. Hampden also received), and in 1831 published a *History of the Jews* which "evaded or minimized the miraculous" (*DNB*). Most important for this Prologue on the doctrinal milieu of *Parochial Sermons*, Milman's *History of Christianity under the Empire* (1840) occasioned Newman's severely critical essay, "Milman's View of Christianity." Newman objects that this author presents Christ's religion "as a secular fact, to the exclusion of all theological truth," for Milman writes "as a Socinian or Unitarian *would* write, whether he will or not" (*Essays & Studies*, II, 219, 231). For example, the Socinian denies Christ's divinity and atonement, which "are not external facts," but admits His humanity and crucifixion, which "*are* external facts," and he does so because he is "bound by his theory to dwell on the latter" and "slur over the former." Newman objects that by "not stating" what the Scriptures record and the Church teaches, Milman undermines doctrine through silence. Yet he does speak candidly when he believes himself among likeminded friends, those he foresees will dismiss miracles since they are "irreconcilable with our actual experience," have already been rejected by "most Protestant Christians," and are out of touch with "the more subtle and fastidious intelligence of the present times" (*History*, I, 130, as quoted by Newman). By applying rationalistic principles to Christian belief, Milman expects to "reconcile the faith of eighteen centuries and the infidelity of the nineteenth." To accept his bad example of reductive interpretation would be to find Christianity "melt away in our hands like snow" (*E & S*, II, 247). Does Milman offer anything positive? Yes he does, since he celebrates the power of human reason—-to which a denatured Christian vocabulary imparts a pleasant feeling tone that infuses the heart with "those sentiments of dependence, of gratitude, of love to God, without which human society must fall to ruin, and the human mind, in humiliating desperation, suspend all its noble activity, and care not to put forth its sublime and eternal energies" (*History*, I, 132, as quoted by Newman in *E & S*, II, 235). Milman's religious views mirror Wordsworth's, for both are amorphously fervent in their religious sentiments, and both accept the Candle of the Lord as the touchstone of truth.

The displacement of doctrine by religious feeling seen in Wordsworth and Milman has been closely evaluated in H. N. Fairchild's study of religious trends in English poetry. Throughout the nineteenth century, "overtly romantic revolt against Christianity" was rare, while "the gradual, mainly unconscious, and. . . . never quite complete romanticizing of Christianity from within by its own declared adherents" (*Christianity and Romanticism in the Victorian Era*, 16–17) was rampant. Though the change was gradual, the difference between the slow alteration assisted by the Milmans of the time and the more candid pronouncements of that small group of distinguished poets who were attempting "to formulate personal religions" in their poetry was not a difference in direction, but only in speed and degree of completeness.

The Milmans and Hampdens of the nineteenth century repudiated the orthodox dogma which Newman was committed to defending, and doing so they unwittingly heralded the new conception of literature which was soon to emerge. The broadly inclusive conception that Dr. Johnson and Coleridge shared included everything in written form regardless of artistic merit, but in the Victorian period this view was displaced by a narrower definition in which artistic merit is the prerequisite for admission. E. D. Hirsch finds "no example of the word in its present, aesthetic connotation before the 1850s," and if Hirsch is right, the definitional narrowing of literature came about for a practical reason. The Victorians invented "literature," "science" and "art" because

> they were the first to require these interrelated conceptions, while the props of revealed religion grew ever weaker as foundations for their spiritual world. "Art" and "literature" are secularized conceptions which embrace writers of the most divergent religious and ethical persuasions within a unified humanistic orientation. 50

The implication is that literature was redefined to foster civil discourse between individuals of differing spiritual convictions by limiting their discourse, by common consent as it were, within a secular dimension. As a result, those born into that definition would find it self-evident that *Parochial Sermons* could not be literature, for it boasts no rhetorical fireworks which might earn it a marginal place. In Basil Willey's terms, the objective domains of knowledge that include theology and philosophy having been rejected in favor of subjective conviction figured by the Candle of the Lord, the religious impulse moved away from a doctrinal faith and migrated towards literature. This shift has been well documented by Fairchild, who demonstrates that English poetry becomes less doctrinally-based to the extent that it becomes increasingly more self-referential. In his final volumes Fairchild necessarily abandons the history-of-ideas emphasis with which he had begun, because he has to discuss "a period within which poetry itself is the only religion possessed by many poets" (Vol. V, ix).

In Newman's day, the most articulate spokesman for the transitional move from objective dogma to subjective belief is Matthew Arnold, who advocates turning Christianity into literature (*Lit. and Dogma* (1873, 1883); *Last Essays on Church and Rel.* (1877)). He calls Christianity "immortal" and grants it "eternal truth" and a "boundless future," yet complains that the popular religion of England continues to conceive of the birth, ministry and death of Jesus as being "steeped in prodigy, brimful of miracle;—*and miracles do not happen*" (*L & D,* 146). Arnold not only dismisses belief in a supernatural realm of being but contemptuously rejects dogmatic language (*"persons," "substance," "godhead . . ."*) designed to articulate Christian doctrines, none of which offensive terms have "anything at all to do with what Jesus said or meant" (*L & D,* 311). He advocates understanding the "familiar language" of religion to be poetry, for "such was also the practice of Jesus." Finally, because England always follows the lead of the Continent, and intellectuals there have thoroughly repudiated doctrinal religion, it is foolishness for the English to hold onto what the *Zeitgeist* has already dismissed (*Last Essays,* 137, 151).

If one uses as a line of distinction between religious and secular mindsets the contrast between belief in what God has revealed and disbelief because reason has not shown it to be true, one could position Catholics, Anglicans and Dissenters together on the same side of that line, because whatever their disagreements on particular points, they are all people of faith. Their response to *Parochial Sermons* testifies to their unanimity in that regard, since Newman's readers have come from all of these differing persuasions. When William Copeland—the friend who represented him with the publisher Rivington when the collection was reissued in 1868—wrote telling him that the volumes were selling well and that Dissenters, too, were buying them, Newman was not astonished. As he wrote Copeland, "It did not surprise me to hear that Dissenters have bought my volumes. I have at various times had letters from men among them . . . who had told me, that, without accepting my ecclesiastical principles, not a few fraternized with me as far as ethical and religious sentiments went" (*L & D*, XXIV, 177). Not so with the Wordsworths, the Milmans and Arnolds of Newman's time or our own, whose intellectual position has triumphed. Academics today think Newman a minor figure in nineteenth-century studies, and his very vocabulary has helped exclude him from higher estimation. Mark Pattison is right to say Newman's resolute purpose was

> to have nothing in common with the liberals and Romantics who now stand in print on either side of him in the anthologies . . . [his] hostility to modernism was so pervasive that he chose not even to speak the language of liberalism, on the theory that to adopt an enemy's language is already to have conceded a major point. Liberalism wants to discuss knowledge; Newman prefers to talk about dogma . . . The modern world wants to examine rationality; Newman would rather investigate Socinianism. The very words he chose to discuss modern problems . . . made his thoughts inaccessible to the great majority of modern readers whose only vocabulary is that of Romanticism or liberalism. 53–4

Yet for all that, *Parochial Sermons* still attracts readers. For example, the novelist Muriel Spark, a great fan of the sermons, describes Newman's voice as one that "never fails to start up, radioactive from the page, however musty the physical book." Newman's "reasoning is so pure that it is revolutionary in form. He does not go forward from point to point; he leads the mind inward, probing the secret place of the subject at hand. You can never anticipate, with Newman, what he is leading up to." His constant aim was "the psychological penetration of moral character, and he achieved it" (*The Critic*, XXII No. 6 (*June-July, 1964*), 28). Spark became a Catholic convert through the influence of Newman's sermons, yet her appreciation stresses not the dogma that he presents but the literary qualities that give delight, such as in Shelley's phrase have power "to pierce the guarded wit,/ And pass into the panting heart beneath/ With lightning and with music" (*Adonais*, 102–04).

CHAPTER 1

Newman and His Reader

In "Voice as Summons for Belief," Walter J. Ong, S. J. discusses the reciprocal relationship between a speaker and his hearers, noting that "voice demands . . . taking the part of the other within who is not ourselves." While what he calls belief as opinion employs language only as the vehicle for transferring information, belief as faith "dwells in words and feeds on them" because they are "manifestations of persons" (55, 57). Newman's sermons are like that, because in them he tries to bring home to others some truth, doctrine, principle or sentiment as forcefully as he has already "brought it home" to himself ("University Preaching," 198–9). He and they "dwell in words" so that together they can collaborate in the shared apprehension of a common insight, situation, danger or opportunity. To do so, Newman must have the ability to enter into his hearers' way of looking at things and present his reflections in a manner which touches a chord in them.

Newman's success at entering into the characteristic ways of thinking of his contemporaries was recognized very early on. His nephew James Mozley, speaking not from personal affection but from what he had "heard and observed everywhere, from the natural, incidental, unconscious remarks" of many individuals, has described Newman's genius for understanding viewpoints other than his own. That, for instance, of the tradesman, his mind focused wholly upon his earthly occupation while the unseen world gradually fades and vanishes to his view. With a comprehensive empathy, Newman grasps "the whole influence of the world on the imagination; the weight of example; the force of repetition; the way in which maxims, rules, sentiments, by being simply sounded in the ear from day to day, seem to prove themselves, and make themselves believed by being often heard." This empathetic capacity is important for the sermonist because, by understanding the frame of mind, he is better able to lead the person caught in its powerful grip to realize its inadequacy and the danger that it poses. As Mozley testifies, Newman

> enters into the ordinary common states of mind just in the same way. He is most consoling, most sympathetic. He sets before persons their own feelings with such truth of detail, such natural expressive touches, that they seem not to be ordinary states of mind which everybody has, but very peculiar ones; for he and the reader seem to be the only two persons in the world that have them in common. Here is the point. Persons look into Mr. Newman's sermons and see their own thoughts in them. (quoted in Church, 139–41)

C. F. Harrold takes a somewhat different view of Newman's talent for picturing the essential contours of others' thoughts, one which emphasizes the auditor's fear of being found out in his "deepest personal secrets." Harrold remarks on Newman's "habit of appearing to be considering some general subject and at the same time of being about to point to an individual hearer and saying 'Thou art the man for whom these words are intended.' This feature of Newman's sermons has been noted by more than one listener. It kept the congregation in a nerve-tingling suspense, and sent it inward upon itself in a feverish sense of shame" (323). Now as an historical fact, such feverish passion would have occurred in some instances for some members of his live audience, and those who so responded probably had good reason for feeling such agitation, but there is no textual evidence that Newman's intent was to terrorize, humiliate and shame his audience. To the contrary, he avoids doing that, for what religious benefit of a lasting nature could be derived from frightening his auditors out of their wits? And yet it certainly is part of his strategy to hover between descriptions of the worldly man's spiritually obtuse conduct and the likelihood that some of his hearers will be moved to recognize in those descriptions similar faults of their own. Harrold's 'Thou art the man' alludes to the prophet Nathan's design for puncturing King David's complacence over having invented a cover-up to conceal adultery and murder, a strategy which hinges upon the indirection of telling David the story about a poor man whose pet lamb was taken and butchered by a wealthy scoundrel (II *Samuel*, 12:1–7), thereby provoking the hot indignation which Nathan deftly deflects towards the king's self-condemnation. Using indirection to find direction out is Newman's strategy as well, with the caveat that he always takes pains to avoid direct accusation, knowing that it generally provokes resentment and denial instead of prompting self-accusal. Hence, Newman's visionary georgic helps his auditors to recognize the real condition of their lives when measured against Christian ideals which no one's aims and actions can perfectly fulfil.

Newman, then, has the capacity to understand others and address them with candor and tact. What more does a visionary georgic require? It needs not simply a design adequate for the presentation of its central important truth, but also a purpose related to that essential message yet not identical with it, that is, a reason for presenting that content to those readers. In this regard a comparison of *Parochial Sermons* with the other visionary georgics we have discussed helps to clarify its distinctive nature. *De rerum natura*, for example, is not well described as a long scientific philosophical anthropological treatise in verse, though it can easily be mistaken for one. Rather, it is a long, complex re-education program intended to bring to the truth those who have been brainwashed into fearing death and the gods' punishment of their sins. That is Lucretius' purpose, and the work's organization is such as he thought would be adequate for the task. As Diskin Clay summarizes its structure, the poem consists of "three units of two books each," the first unit providing a foundation for the rest by presenting "the main theoretical propositions of Epicurus' physics." Books III and IV discuss the chief problems to be overcome, "the fear of death and the visions (*simulacra*) that seem to guarantee the unsettling belief in an afterlife and an immortal soul," and the last two books "treat the world and the phenomena in it which provoke wonder, anxiety, and a belief in the gods" (35).

Clearly, that is a considerable amount of ground to cover, and few readers, particularly those who are skeptical or even resentful of the Epicurean postulates they are asked to accept will attend to its lengthy argument without being either forced or cajoled into doing so. How Lucretius manages that can be seen by recalling John Dryden's delightful description of Lucretius "assuming absolute command not only over his vulgar reader, but even his patron Memmius. For he is always bidding him attend, as if he had the rod over him; and using a magisterial authority, while he instructs him." Memmius is the intra-textual stand-in for the rest of us, who enjoy seeing him suffering his beating because we savor the energy of the Lucretius voice tolerating no nonsense from a potentially indifferent or skeptical pupil, and we attend more closely for seeing Memmius punished. Says Dryden, Lucretius "seems to disdain all manner of replies, and is so confident of his cause that he is beforehand with his antagonists, urging for them whatever he imagined they could say, and leaving them as he supposes, without an objection for the future. All this too, with so much scorn and indignation, as if he were assured of the triumph before he entered into the lists" (Preface to *Sylvae*, 1685). One should not take too literally Dryden's dramatizing of reader relations in *De rerum natura* as a battle, for Lucretius, a dramatist in his own right, knows what he is doing. He understands that so dauntingly protracted a presentation as his runs the danger of losing the reader who is not regularly shaken up, either insulted or entertained into attention. And that strategy works because Lucretius has the polished skills of a vaudeville entertainer, not despite but because of his seriousness of purpose. Aside from the reiterated Memmius abuse, we encounter the periodic set pieces decrying the harm done to people by religion, beginning with Lucretius' description of Agamemnon's ritual sacrifice of his beloved daughter Iphigenia. Nor are such tirades his only device for re-activating attention by human interest interludes. Although this is not the place to catalogue his entire repertoire, we can look briefly at a single comic routine, one that Mark Twain would have liked, featuring a crowd of souls standing around at conception or birth waiting to hitch a ride in some available body—a view that Lucretius calls "utter nonsense," but one that allows him to enliven his serious point that the soul, as well, is made of atoms and expires at the body's death: "immortal souls waiting for mortal bodies/ in numberless numbers, or running races to see/ which should be first, which favored to slip in!/ Or do the souls have contracts, signed and sealed:/ 'The soul that swoops in first shall have first chance/ to enter: no pushing or shoving, no argument!'" (III.776–83).

Turning attention to Wordsworth's *Prelude*, we find it organized as a quasi-narrative, for it is the portrait of a would-be artist seeking his vocation, a portrait drawn by abstracting from the whole personal history those elements which are pertinent to his theme: delight in nature in childhood, uneasy residence at Cambridge, a walking tour of the Alps, his disappointment over the French revolution followed by the temptation to "yield up moral questions in despair" (XI, 301–05), then the later recovery to inner tranquillity, the recognition of his vocation as a poet, and the concluding lyrical grandeur of his ascent of Mount Snowden. That the poem is a portrait of the artist trying to discover himself does not preclude its being a visionary georgic, although it raises the problem of recognizing it as one. Wordsworth is so wholly intent upon reconstructing his recollections of agony and grandeur and interpreting their significance for himself, that one could easily be skeptical that the poem has a georgic's function, which is to instruct its audience in some practical way. Instead of abusing the Friend who represents the reader, as we have seen Lucretius do, Wordsworth excludes this intratextual auditor from *The Prelude's* recollective activity, while nevertheless referring to that shadow of a shade now and again lest he disappear from the work altogether. That is what one ought to expect, given what Wordsworth has to say. For although we may have all of us one human heart, as he puts it elsewhere, one's recollections are one's own since personal experience is unique, and those experiences are the sunken treasure Wordsworth labors to recover from the depths of memory in order to articulate and comprehend.

It is not simply that Wordsworth lacks the negative capability to join Keats on the window sill pecking in the gravel with the sparrow, although he does indeed lack it. It is rather that he ignores his audience so unwaveringly because, in his

Protestant conviction, he knows that the inner light of the Lord's candle shines most brightly if one figurally retires to a private room, pulls down the shades and reflects in isolation on what others must think about for themselves. This is the activity modelled by the poem, and we recall the passage which states it outright: "Here must Thou be, O Man!/ Power to thyself; no Helper hast thou here;/ Here keepest thou in singleness thy state" (XIV, 209–11). While Lucretius has a complex and unwelcome doctrine to render palatable for his reader, Wordsworth's doctrine, implicit in the extended example of his own life, has no defined content beyond the faith that a certain kind of heroic self-concentration by the individual can reveal that elusive "something ever more about to be" grandeur lodged within or created by the effort of one's imagination working upon the raw materials of ordinary experience.

Returning to Ong's postulate that "voice demands . . . taking the part of the other within who is not ourselves," what range of styles regarding empathy with its readers can we discover in the visionary georgic? Aside from either abusing or amusing his reader to renew attention, Lucretius offers him the very seductive flattery of coaxing him to join that happy few whose acceptance of Epicurus' doctrines proves them to be smarter than others: "nothing is sweeter than to dwell in peace/ high in the well-walled temple of the wise/ whence looking down we may see other men/ wavering, wandering, seeking a way of life,/ with wit against wit . . . straining night and day,/ to rise to the top of the heap" (II,7–13). Adopting a very different relationship with his readers, Wordsworth expects their hearts, simply through the force of example his poem provides, to begin the self-appropriation through self-reflection which is the author's up-dated response to Milton's theology. As for Newman, the right place to begin is by recognizing that he does not teach his readers in the sense of instructing them about unfamiliar things, for they were all raised in Anglican families and have long known the doctrines and services of the church, along with the Old and New Testament documents which lie behind and have been incorporated within the church's prayers and services. In that key respect Newman's georgic differs from those of Lucretius and Wordsworth, who feel the need, or rather recognize the necessity, of instructing their audiences.

What Newman's readers truly need is encouragement and direction towards realizing in their lives the doctrines which they have known since childhood, but which in the absence of reflection lie fallow within them. Newman's task is to help them dwell in the words they are familiar with in order that, by feeding upon them, they might incorporate their living meaning into themselves. It is performance skills, not information *per se*, that they lack. At the root of the challenge Newman hopes to make them rise to is this, that the word they need to dwell in and feed upon is Christ, the Word of God, for Christianity is unlike anything in the natural world, an incorporation into God become man, through the invisible aid of the

Holy Spirit. Newman's auditors do not need to be scolded about adultery and murder, they need to be taught how to pray. And his preeminent qualification as a sermonist is that he recognizes that need and tries to satisfy it.

There is a sense in which every one of Newman's sermons is the same sermon over again because they all seek to effect the same goal, yet they do not blur together. What keeps them from doing so is the fact that every sermon makes a single point, and because each sermon stands apart from the others in this way, sermons which make *related* points lend themselves to Newman's procedure of assembling them into clusters of thematically related sermons for volume publication, the typical pattern being that a volume contains four such clusters averaging six sermons each. Every sermon begins with its own scriptural epigraph and thematic title, along with the particular fact, problem, insight or paradox which helps establish the sermon's trajectory of exploration. If a single substantive quality is characteristic of Newman's approach to his readers, it is commonality of reflection between speaker and hearer, mutuality of exploration of the theme, paradox, problem or fact that is explored.

In contrast to Lucretius' bullying and Wordsworth's disengagement from his audience, Newman's voice invites his readers to participate in their common effort to better understand themselves and their faith. For example, when the sermonist interrupts his forward progress to raise an objection to the direction his own thought has been taking, one senses that he is raising it not only because he anticipates his auditor's silently doing so, but because he himself feels the objection's force and wishes to bring it into focal attention, where it can enrich the texture of thinking and help keep it from sidetracking into oversights on its progress towards insight. In a Newman sermon one senses both the force of intellectual competence and the undertone of self-effacing humility which gives evidence that he is neither showing us up nor showing off, and this double quality of the speaker's voice is reassuring to his readers, who do not mind joining him on a journey but hate to be lectured at.

The first volume of *Parochial Sermons* is a training program for young adults, one that prepares them to live their Christianity fully and fervently. I have selected eight of the volume's twenty-six sermons, two from each of its four sermon clusters, to illustrate Newman's relations with his readers. The first of these, "Holiness Necessary for Future Blessedness," leaps across the lives of his auditors, who are only now beginning to live, and focuses upon the need to prepare early for getting into heaven. Newman opens the sermon with the unobjectionable fact that "to make sinful creatures holy was the great end which our Lord had in view in taking upon Him our nature" and immediately thereafter states an objection against it: "some one may ask 'Why is it that holiness is a necessary qualification,'" as though it were comparable to a train ticket or an admissions pass. By stating that objection,

Newman deftly establishes the rift between the history of redemption's purpose and the complaint that it would be more merciful of God to save us just as we are——the gap through which he will lead his hearers toward a deeper understanding of religious reality.

His next step is to define holiness. To be holy is "to take pleasure in keeping God's commandments" and "to live habitually as in the sight of the world to come," such that holiness is essentially related to personal pleasure and the delight of happy expectations. His auditor's unconsidered notion of pleasure would most likely be closer to sensual gratification and being well liked, but Newman quietly challenges them on that score, and while it is asking much of the young to require of them the imaginative leap of having "broken the ties of this life" when those ties have as yet barely been formed, he does ask it. To understand Newman's relations with his readers it is essential that we attend to pronoun reference, i.e., how and to whom he attributes the views and actions his sermons describe. For example, the question why holiness should be necessary is asked by an unspecified "some one" who might so object, yet when Newman is completing the orienting interrogative phase of the sermon's opening, he replaces that "some one" by "we," asking "Why cannot we be saved without possessing such a frame and temper of mind?" What has happened here? The answer is that the first irreverent question's latent querulousness has been innoculated against irreverence by the fact that "we" now ask it, not as a challenge but "to enlarge our insight into our own condition and prospects," which is a devotional exercise. After that point, pronoun reference shifts back once again, to "a man of unholy life," a description tacitly excluding members of Newman's audience. Were such a man "suffered to enter heaven, *he would not be happy there,*" which explodes the admissions pass conception of what getting into heaven involves. Then, pronoun reference returns to the inclusive "we" that accuses no one, though it makes room for personal failings: "We are apt to deceive ourselves, and to consider heaven a place like this earth." Having established the trajectory as he needs it aimed to pursue his exposition, Newman remains with the "we" referent for quite some time: "We see that in this world . . . Hence we are led to act as if . . . But an opinion like this is refuted as soon as put into words," because heaven is not like this world. Having explored what heaven cannot be like, Newman quotes four verses from *Revelation* describing heaven and concludes that "these passages from St. John are sufficient to remind us of many others," and thereby to his readers he assigns the cooperative task of recalling other verses for themselves.

Because the sermon needs another push in the direction that he wishes it to take, Newman goes beyond St. John's description by likening heaven to a less visionary reality: "Heaven then is not like this world; I will say what it is much more like,——*a church.* For in a place of public worship no language of this world is heard," language being taken to mean discussion of trade, politics and the like. At this juncture the sermon stands to profit by another negative example, and therefore reference shifts away from "we" to "an irreligious man" who could not "spiritually see" God in a church. "Were such a man to come hither, who had suffered his mind to grow up in its own way, as nature or chance determined" [and as no member of the audience is accused of doing, let it be noted], "he would find no real pleasure here." By analogy, such a man would in heaven find himself "an isolated being" with nothing to make him "feel at home," and the loneliness would be unendurable. Having described the poor fellow's discomfiture, Newman glides away from that unfortunate "he" to the rest of us, the "we" who by now surely ought to know better. It would be incorrect to assert that Newman now indicts the reader, but it is certainly the case that the insulating space that separates the foolish "he" from the favored "we" grows less wide as the sermonist continues to explore the mental state of the person with "narrow views and earthly aims, a low standard of duty, and a benighted conscience, a mind contented with itself, and unresigned to God's will." Such a person "would feel as little pleasure, at the last day, at the words, 'Enter into the joy of thy Lord,' as it does now at the words, 'Let us pray.'" Of course Newman cannot know whether any such person is present and hearing him say these words. If any such auditor feels the discomfort of tacit accusal, it must come from conscience, for only the person's inner voice monitoring his conduct and judging it could point a finger at him and make the accusation stick.

As with the Italian sonnet, which describes its focal problem in the octave and then turns to the problem-solving sestet which concludes the poem, so a Newman sermon often has an equivalent "turn" near its middle, after which the practical advice that is the heart of a georgic is given. In "Holiness Necessary for Future Blessedness" that turn occurs when Newman writes "Now then I will mention two important truths which seem to follow from what has been said" in the expository section, and keeping that promise brings him to sermon's end. The first truth, "if a certain state of heart and affections" is required to enter heaven, "our *actions* will avail for our salvation" so far as they help to produce that frame of mind. Second, "if holiness be not merely the doing a certain number of good actions" but is instead the "inward character" fostered by doing them, "how far distant from that holiness are the multitude of men." These truths lead into the peroration urging his hearers to exert themselves vigorously, given the obstacles they face and the importance of mastering them:

> I fear there are those, who, if they dealt faithfully with their consciences, would be obliged to own that they had not made the service of God their first concern; that their obedience, so to call it, has been a matter of course, in which the heart has had no part; that they have acted uprightly in worldly matters chiefly for the sake of their worldly interest. 1.12

Newman cannot swear that any in his audience fit that description, but he fears it, and therefore brings it to the attentions of those who are able to know themselves, and to act on that knowledge.

As we saw Newman clarify the nature of heaven by first denying its comparability to any earthly experience and by then comparing it to a church service, in a similar manner "Self-Denial the Test of Religious Earnestness" presents its readers an extended analogy that is pursued with much the same vigor. Adopting St. Paul's statement "Now it is high time to awake out of sleep" as the sermon's epigraph, and taking sleep to signify "a state of insensibility to things as they really are in God's sight," Newman uses the sleep analogy to awaken his readers to the problematic condition of religion in England. He begins by describing for them the conventional panoramic painting of heaven and earth, with God on His throne at the top of the canvas "trying the reins and heart" of his creatures below, surrounded by multitudes of angels and saints, some of which, further down on the canvas, are "by their errands of mercy connecting this lower world with His courts above." Meanwhile, His Church on earth heralds the good news "with power to individual minds," so that "the truths of religion circulate through the world almost as the light of day," which ought to awaken its inhabitants. Such is the state of a Christian country, but what of its citizens? "They are *asleep*." We can tell that because "they see and hear as people in a dream," they mix up God's word with "their own idle imaginings" and they suppose that "their happiness consists in continuing as they are." Though Newman's readers are spectators of the picture he has drawn, they well understand that they too are implicated in the figural somnolence which has been charged.

Such a major investment of sermonic energy as this dramatic introduction can be justified only if it engages the reader's attention productively, and for that to happen Newman must validate the implication that his readers, too, harbor "such a vague, defective extravagant" notion of God's truth "as a man sees when he is asleep." He will need to activate the sleep analogy by showing its truth, which requires that he demonstrate spiritual somnolence in the conduct of the English people. Doing so is the second stage of this sermon's expository movement, its survey of "the circumstances of these times" which make religious sincerity particularly difficult. Being certain that one's faith is sincere was easier when following Christ was a capital crime and martyrdom was always near at hand. Now, however, when the governing classes are enthusiastic in their support of religion, it is harder to know whether one "really acts on faith, or from a desire of this world's advantages." How, then, can we probe our own heart "after the manner of Him who, from His throne above, tries it with an Almighty Wisdom." Self-deception is the difficulty, for although truth has the power to make one "profess it in words," when the time for action comes, "instead of obeying *it*," one can inadvertently substitute "some idol in the place of it." Therefore, when religion stands in good repute, "a cautious mind will feel anxious" lest some counterfeit has subtly intruded itself.

Having first dramatized and then validated the sleep metaphor, Newman makes the "turn" to practical advice with the question "How then shall we try ourselves?" Absenting any foolproof trial, self-denial is a reliable touchstone. It was the "great evidence" given by the first disciples, who are still our models for conduct. And Jesus Himself provides the appropriate counsel in words Newman's audience can dwell in and feed upon ("Whosoever doth not bear his cross and come after Me . . ."). Descending to specific strategies, the sermon suggests that we focus upon our own "besetting infirmities," which will not be adultery and murder but, say, over-fondness for amusement, ill-temper or an ill-controlled tongue. Not least of such infirmities—mentioned late and softened by generality—are those "bad passions, of which they [not we, or you, but "they"] "are ashamed, yet are overcome." Here is an unnamed vice which could explode silently within the private sensibilities of some young males present, raising a potentially corrective consternation there. Every one has something to work on, yet whatever one's self-denials, they must be practiced daily, for occasional actions do not establish sound habit patterns: "Try yourself daily in little deeds, to prove that your faith is more than a deceit."

The two sermons we have examined so far provide their readers visionary perspective, i.e., ways of seeing their religious situation more clearly, the practical advice they offer near sermon's end being ancillary to the situational analysis. In contrast, the two sermons which represent the volume's second cluster are entirely devoted to giving the practical advice that people in certain circumstances need. For example, "The Religious Use of Excited Feelings" draws from St. Luke's account of the cured demoniac a lesson for those who, "having neglected religion in their early youth, at length begin to have serious thoughts, try to repent, and wish to serve God better than hitherto, though they do not know how to set about it." Their commonest error is to mistake the powerful emotion which has overcome them to be religion's essence, when it should be recognized as a God-given aid which removes "from the *beginnings* of obedience its *grievousness*" by providing the strong impulse which can "carry us over the first obstacles." Because such emotion springs from novelty, it soon wears off, and therefore one should "make use of" it immediately by performing some charitable act for a person in need; doing so can carry you "across a gulf, to which your ordinary strength is not equal." Doing something for another person through the impulse of transient emotion can set going an obedience to God which is based on action, not feeling.

After having reversed his commonest organizational procedure by giving his practical advice first, Newman asks his readers "how do men usually conduct themselves" when overcome by repentence generated emotion. He then presents a lengthy taxonomy of erroneous responses to such feelings in a section of the sermon dominated by the distancing pronoun "they," which makes Newman's auditors the guiltless spectators rather than perpetrators of error. "They," such men, "look upon the turbid zeal and feverish devotion" prompted by recoil from their own former "corrupt state of mind" as

> the substance and real excellence of religion. They think that to be thus agitated is to be religious; they indulge themselves in these warm feelings for their own sake, resting in them as if they were then engaged in a religious exercise, and boasting of them as if they were an evidence of their own exalted spiritual state; not *using them* (the one only thing they ought to do), using them as an incitement to *deeds* of love, mercy, truth, meekness, holiness. 1.118

Like Nathan describing for King David another man's vicious folly, Newman displays a masque-like processional sequence in which bad actions progress towards worse, for "having neglected to turn their feelings into principles by acting upon them, they have no inward strength to overcome the temptation to live as the world, which continually assails them." There except for prompt action, Newman cautions his auditors, they themselves might go. He nudges them towards discovering for themselves the difference between the power of present emotion and the efficacy of religious habit.

Such men as he is here characterizing, detecting their own slippage into a worse condition, "are alarmed, and look around for a means of recovering themselves," but, scorning lowly obedience along with charity and sobriety, they grasp at "potent stimulants to sustain" the error which has by now become habitual. The "better sort" among them, those having "something of religious principle in their hearts," nonetheless cannot avoid being "distressed and alarmed at their own tranquillity, which they suppose is a bad sign" because it signifies that their religion is evaporating. Still others despise their former state in life and suppose themselves "called to some high and singular office in the Church." The moral Newman draws from this sad spectacle is clear: one should secure God's favor "by *acting* upon" the transient excitements that repentance produces, since "they are the instruments of His spirit" to be used well. These will soon enough die away, yet "if they die, it is but as blossom changes into fruit, which is far better."

The other advice-focused representative of the second sermon group, "Profession Without Hypocrisy," is dedicated to prayer, the difficulties of praying well. Here, instead of picturing a worst-case scenario as in the previous sermon, Newman's procedure is to speak with the tender solicitude of a friend allaying one's fears in a delicate instance of distressing weakness. Having in a previous sermon solemnly warned against hypocrisy, he softens his earlier sternness by taking a gentler stance, "lest timid consciences should be frightened" into accusing themselves of nonperformance, when truly no one can pray so well as he should. He observes that "men profess without feeling and doing, or are hypocrites, in nothing so much as in their prayers," and therefore he enlarges upon "the case of prayer, to explain what I do *not* mean by hypocrisy." When people use devotional words but without attending to them, without "worthily entering into" their meaning, they can easily think themselves like the Pharisees and imagine that it would be better to avoid the Church's prayers and make more suitable ones of their own. When these too disappoint them because they are "as unable to fix their thoughts as before," such persons may conclude that they ought not try to pray at all, except when they are specially moved by the Holy Spirit to do so.

Clearly, Newman opens by describing problems in prayer with which all can identify because spiritual dryness, the failure to enter into the meanings of the words uttered in prayer, are common. With the gentleness of a good mother calming her distressed child and talking the little one out of disabling self-disappointment, he sets to his task, insisting from the outset that attentive prayer is a habit, and habits must be formed; "no one *begins* with" having heart and mind invested in his prayers, but "after many trials and a long schooling" one learns to "fix his mind" more steadily. Seasons of attentive devotion "come by fits and starts," which is to be expected because "no habit is formed at once," a truth which "impatient men" neglect to consider. Newman employs the distancing "they" pronoun to catalogue a number of common errors some of which he knows his hearers will have experienced though he avoids saying so—-such as hoping to become more attentive by focusing their minds upon "the more sacred doctrines of the Gospel, and thus rousing and constraining their souls," which does well enough for a time, but when the novelty has passed, they are on their knees again, still without a strategy for praying any better.

After a number of such close-hand descriptions of the problems encountered in prayer, Newman delivers his advice. He draws consolation and strength for his audience even from their failures, which in most cases are only partial. Of course if one's mind wanders from start to finish, then it is clearly not the length of the church service which is at fault. But when a person is able to "fix his attention for a time, during the early part of the service," Newman would have him "reflect that even this degree of attention was not always his own," and Christians who have come that far can, with time and practice, go farther, and eventually pay attention "through the whole service."

As for the difficulty of entering into the meaning of prayers when in fact we are attentive to them, Newman calls this the distinctive difficulty of "the tender conscience," the person who "will ask, 'How is it possible I *can* rightly use the solemn words which occur in the prayers?'" Those he names "confident objectors," who dismiss "set prayer" as being most often "a mere formal service" wherein the heart is not involved, "are silent here" because they do not feel the difficulty of "having to address the God of heaven" worthily. Newman reminds those of tender conscience that, as they know, Christ is the only way "open to sinners," and that the best we can do is understand our "insincerity, and shallowness of mind," of which the inability to pray well is but one facet. Yet when we do our best, the Holy Spirit "maketh intercession for us with plaints unutterable," an insight that will be our strongest consolation. The single case of difficulties in prayer is sufficient to illustrate "Profession Without Hypocrisy," because what is true there is true of all.

While the first two sermon clusters of Volume 1 speak to the Christian's personal performance in response to the Gospel, the sermons that represent the third cluster, "Religious Faith Rational" and "The Christian Mysteries," do something different. They provide confidence building information intended to help the Christian stand firm against the age's tendency to make intellect the arbiter of faith, by clarifying the limits of human reason with regard to divine revelation. Recognizing that his hearers can no longer live by trusting the testimony of parents and elders but must make their own religious decisions, and must do so within an intellectual milieu that increasingly expresses disregard or contempt for realities that are unseen, Newman anticipates the process of intimidation by which the young can be cowed into thinking that the beliefs they once held reduce to an unreflective, a childish prejudice. Attack is the argumentative stance that Newman adopts here, for error must be faced and shown to be chimerical, not least because seeing error thus exposed helps to build the confidence that young Christians need.

Newman begins his argument by briefly summarizing two inaccurate descriptions of religious faith which his audience will already have encountered, whether in their reading or in casual conversations. Some serious men who ought to know better have described Christian faith as "different in kind from everything that affects and influences us in matters of this world," and have said that it is therefore wrong "to compare it with any of our natural principles or feelings." Such persons unwittingly "lead others, who wish an excuse for their own irreligious lives," to describe faith more perniciously, calling it "extravagant and irrational, as if it were a mere fancy or feeling, which some persons had and others not." Newman's position is that while the objects of religious faith are indeed "unheard and unthought of elsewhere," it is not true that faith is never acted upon except in religious matters, for we constantly act on trust in the testimony of others; "it is the things believed, not the act of believing them, which is peculiar to religion." Having presented that principle, Newman exemplifies it by considering our common experience, which refutes on the one hand the argument that religious faith is incomparable with anything else in our lives, and on the other hand that it is "extravagant and irrational."

Given the narrow scope of what we know from first-hand experience, we have to rely upon the testimony of others in order to live, and all of us are reconciled to that fact. It is only in religious matters that trust or faith is deemed irrational by "the proud and sinful." Newman is not engaging in name-calling in lieu of argument but is instead describing an attitude. Attitude is the key, for those who reject the claims of religion instinctively wish to justify their position by raising themselves above people of faith, which they do through the preemptive characterization of calling them irrational. Attitude preemptively answers the question "what are our reasons for believing" the Gospel, the scoffer posing the question "in a scoffing way" because he does not believe. But, says Newman, turning from the proud and sinful man to his own attentive audience,

> if a man inquires sincerely, wishing to find the truth, waiting on God humbly, yet perplexed at the deeds of scorners and daring blasphemers, and at hearing their vain reasonings, and not knowing what to think or say about them, let him consider the following remarks. 1.197

He is telling them do not be intimidated by the confidence of brash nay-sayers whose intellects are governed by self-serving vanity, which scorns to accept God's Word because doing so would depress them in their own esteem.

Unmasking their motives for the sake of his hearers, Newman says that unbelievers may "pretend" that they have no quarrel with being required to believe, but in fact they do have a quarrel with faith. They reject it because "they do not like dependence," and to escape it have "set up some image of freedom in their minds," a freedom contrary to the "shackles" of having to rely upon the dubious word of an unseen God. Aiming for what he perceives as the chink in his opponents' armor, Newman observes that our obedience is not founded only on the word of the Gospel's ministers, but that "we obey God primarily because we actually feel His presence in our consciences bidding us obey Him." This fact confutes such objectors "on their own ground," for if they claim to trust their own sight and reason more than the word of God's representatives because sight and reason are "their own," "why do they not trust their consciences too? Is not conscience their own?" It is indeed, Newman says, and God gave it to them "to balance the influence of sight and reason," though they will not attend to it since "they love to be their own masters." This perverse love is demonstrated by their becoming angry or scornful whenever conscience is appealed to. Their vaunted reason then falls mute, leaving disturbed passions as their only "champions." Surely, Newman invites his auditors to conclude, these are not reasoning beings whom Christians can trust, nor should anyone be "perplexed and frightened" by their bold words.

While "Religious Faith Rational" counters the attacks of scoffers, "The Christian Mysteries" addresses the latent scoffer within Newman's hearer by rejecting the presumption that the purpose of the intellect is to clarify everything. Such a presumption reveals a mirroring resemblance to the rationalist's rejection of faith for being based upon weak evidence, when it is not the evidence but our intellects which are inadequate. Newman opens with the principle that the illumination given by the Spirit at Pentecost "is not a light accorded to reason," for as Trinity Sunday reminds us, "the Gospel has its mysteries, its difficulties, and secret things, which the Holy Spirit does not remove." The light of Christianity has been given "not that we may know more, but that we may do better," a corrective which goes against the grain of a world wherein knowledge is commonly prized above holiness. Newman notes that there have always been those who have considered mysteries inconsistent with biblical revelation, "and hence they have argued, that no doctrine which was *mysterious* . . . could be contained in Scripture." A better guide, Newman suggests, is Nicodemus, a sincere inquirer who started with surprise on being told he must be born again, yet who did not let incomprehension prevent belief. He felt the temptation but overcame it.

To draw his hearers more fully into the investigation, Newman casts a wide net which gathers a considerable number of phenomena which are mysterious to us because we cannot discover any satisfying explanation for them. Why is there so much pain and suffering in the world, why such terrible accidents and cruel diseases? Why did the Jews' slaughter of unoffending animals persuade God to be gracious to them, and why did He select Israel in particular when He might have taught all nations "by direct revelation, the sin of idol-worship"? Why should Christ's sacrifice have been necessary for our salvation, and, closer to home, why were Newman's auditors born into Christian families living in a Christian country when countless others elsewhere and over the ages have lacked the benefits of baptism and the Gospel truth? After noting many such disturbing inequities which baffle thinking, Newman does two things. First, he points to the limitations of human nature as the insuperable cause of our inadequate understanding, for while "religious truth requires you should be told *something*, your own imperfect nature prevents your knowing *all*." Indeed, the Christian revelation actually increases the mysteries that we face, for religious light throws its shadows across the outlines of religious darkness, as when the revelation of eternal happiness brings with it the news of eternal damnation. Second, Newman assigns a plausible explanation for mystery: "difficulties in revelation are especially given to prove *the reality of our faith*," since they are "stumbling-blocks to proud and unhumbled minds." Newman then exemplifies the trial of faith posed by religious mysteries, by adumbrating the gospel wherein Jesus tells his disciples "Except ye eat the flesh of the Son of Man, and drink his blood," to which many said "This is a hard saying," while Peter responded by asking a question of his own, "Lord, to whom shall we go?" Though his audience have heard the words many times before, presented to them in this sermon stating that "difficulties in revelation are especially given to prove *the reality of our faith,*" they cannot help but find their own faith being put to the test. The situation calls for them to endorse the frame of mind expressed in "Lord, to whom shall we go?" if, like Peter, they are His disciples. On the other hand, knowing that sincere belief is as much the work of diligent efforts over time as are reliable habits, Newman tells his audience it is

> no matter whether we believe doubtingly or not, or know clearly or not, so that *we act* upon our belief. The rest will follow in time; part in this world, part in the next. 1.214

Because effective training programs are built upon a functional progression from initial lessons to concluding advice, we might expect that Volume 1 of *Parochial Sermons* would progress in that way, and so it does. Its first two sermon clusters emphasize the development and testing of religious sincerity and performance, their insistent focus being on individual conduct. Then at mid-volume the focus shifts noticeably away from personal performance towards reflective meditation on the troubled state of Christianity in Newman's time and the challenges that his trainees must anticipate having to face. That change in emphasis is well illustrated if one compares the earlier sermon "Self-Denial the Test of Religious Earnestness" with a later one, "The Religion of the Day." For while they both cover much the same ground, the religious sincerity of the individual is the focus of the first, the corrupt nature of the religion invented by Satan to satisfy the attitudes, assumptions and tastes of the time is the focus of the second.

"The Religion of the Day" begins not with a question intended to verify the sincerity of the sermon's readers, but with a statement of fact intended to prompt historical reflection, so that Newman's audience will appreciate their own place in the history of Christianity, and by doing so be innoculated against the religious errors of their time. "In every age of Christianity" there has been "a *religion of the world,*" which imitates the true religion the better "to deceive the unstable and unwary." This ersatz religion adopts "one or other" of Christianity's characteristics and ignores the rest, then corrupts "even that portion of it which it has exclusively put forward." Thus by a clever slight-of-hand the religion of the world hopes to "explain away the whole." Newman briefly mentions the Arian heresy which in early centuries of the Church led many into error, then describes the "second idol of the true Christ," which predominated during the "rude and fierce" medieval period, when "Satan took the darker side of the Gospel" and used it to shape a "fierce religion" tailored for the time. These historical antecedents are intended to help his audience to grasp their own endangerment by "perhaps a more pernicious" falsehood than those which flourished in earlier centuries.

Having begun the sermon in that manner, Newman will go on to describe in some detail the individual threads of error which have been interwoven to form the false religion of his own time. But before beginning that exposition, he does something which is more important to this chapter's focus on his relations with readers, for instead of helping them recognize hidden faults in themselves, as the earlier portion of the volume does, Newman now treats his readers as equals, as people who can, and indeed must, discover falsehood for themselves. He will, he says, attempt to expose Satan's devices in their own day,

> or rather to suggest some remarks towards its exposure, . . . for the subject is too great and too difficult for an occasion such as the present, and, after all, no one can detect falsehood for another;—every man must do it for himself; we can but *help* each other. 1.311

This is a new attitude towards his reader, one that cannot be discovered earlier in the volume. "Self-Denial the Test of Religious Earnestness," while cognizant of religious error, had been focused upon what James Mozley calls "the whole influence of the world on the imagination; the weight of example; the force of repetition," all those evanescent enablers which make it easier, and perhaps inevitable, for people to drift into the conduct typical of and endorsed by what Newman describes as the religion of the day. But "The Religion of the Day" is wholly focused upon the pernicious substance of that corrupting fabric of religious falsehood.

Newman's was an optimistic century in the sense that his countrymen preferred to see the bright side of a world that was fast becoming a better place through educational advances and scientific progress, along with the spread of civilized attitudes such as the contempt for vices like public drunkenness, rude behavior, "intolerance, bigotry, excess of zeal" and similar disruptions of social amity. The mind had become more cultivated, but at the cost of being gripped by an insatiable demand for "new objects in religion, new systems and plans, new doctrines," and a general dissatisfaction "with things as they are," so that the age was largely driven by the expectation and hope of a general reformation of human society. Having sketched that picture of the country they live in, Newman turns to his audience and asks them, putting Christianity out of their thoughts for the moment, to

> consider whether such a state of refinement . . . is not that to which men might be brought, quite independent of religion, by the mere influence of education and civilization; and then again, whether, nevertheless, this mere refinement of mind is not more or less all that is called religion at this day . . . is it not the case, that Satan has so composed and dressed out what is the mere natural prudence of the human heart . . . as to serve his purposes as the counterfeit of the Truth? 1.313

The remainder of the sermon explores the different ways in which the day's religion appeals to different attitudinal types. To religious people, for example, who think that the elegance and refinement of private life, attended by "beneficent and enlightened acts of state policy," signify "the approaching advent of Christ." Or to those who trust themselves more than God's word, persons of skeptical mind who "lay much stress on works of *Natural Theology*" in the belief that "all religion is contained in these," when in fact the sun, moon and stars declare the glory of God, "but not His *will*." Having surveyed the contemporary situation, Newman begins his concluding paragraph not with performance advice, but with an appeal to his auditors to reflect upon the pernicious corruptions of Christian truth which he has described: "Think of this, I beseech you, my brethren, and lay it to heart, as far as you go with me."

Newman's usual way of beginning a sermon is to pose a question to direct the thinking he invites his audience to share. A final example of how he relates to his readers, "Witnesses of the Resurrection," begins with the question, why did not Christ reveal Himself after His resurrection to all the people, why only to a favored few "witnesses chosen before of God" (*Acts* 10: 40–1)? As the investigation goes forward, a subsidiary question embedded within the initial query begins to emerge, i.e., how does Christ's revealing Himself only to a favored few impinge upon the sermon's auditors? It does so directly, for everything that Newman observes about Christ's preparation of His Apostles to go preach the Gospel to the world applies, in their measure, to the sermon's auditors. They are commissioned by baptism to carry the message into their corner of the world, which they can succeed in doing only through utter conviction and competent preparation. As Christ employed the forty-day post-resurrection period to prepare His Apostles to spread the good news to all nations, *Parochial Sermons'* first volume is in a similar manner devoted to preparing Newman's readers to follow in the Apostles' footsteps.

The social analysis generated by the sermon's opening question is in large part a sustained reflection on human nature in its unredeemed condition, the natural man being as "unstable as water," void of principles which could give him direction and constancy. Only the well-trained few can make a lasting change for the better in the world. And the ordinary course of divine providence includes reliance upon those select few to effect its purposes, for only they have hearts sufficiently free to surrender themselves to God's will. It is never a question of personal brilliance, since "The most excellent gifts of the intellect last but for a season. Eloquence and wit, shrewdness and dexterity, these plead a cause well and propagate it quickly, but it dies with them. It has no root in the hearts of men, and lives not out a generation." In speaking thus, Newman is tacitly warning his readers against succumbing to spiritual pride, the temptation to rely upon their own thinking as the final arbiter of their conduct. The better way, the path towards salvation, is to conform oneself to the scriptural truth that "the foolishness of God is stronger than men." The Apostles in their day heard that truth and accepted it into their hearts, and so can Newman's readers:

We, too, though we are not witnesses of Christ's actual resurrection, are so spiritually. By a heart awake from the dead, and by affections set on heaven, we can as truly and without figure witness that Christ liveth, as they did . . . And thus in a dark world Truth still makes way in spite of the darkness, passing from hand to hand. 1.292–3

CHAPTER 2

Newman's Vision of the Church

"The Stone that Became a Great Mountain"

Newman adopted as the external organizing framework of Volume 2 the Table of Holy Days in the *Book of Common Prayer*, which allowed him to present Anglican Christianity with the wholeness and balance provided by its alternation between the doctrinal feasts and saints' days of the church calendar (Lams, 2004, Ch. 2). But his purpose in doing so is less clear. His specific intent in Volume 2 has yet to be identified, and the key to that lies in the composition dates of the sermons it contains. Newman's practice was to prepare a written text shortly before it was to be orally delivered, afterwards selecting from his store of earlier-preached sermons those he decided to publish, arranging them into the thematic clusters we find in the other five volumes of *Parochial Sermons*. But Volume 2 is different, for while half of its 32 sermons had been delivered from the pulpit, the other half were not written for preaching to his Oxford congregation but for direct inclusion in the printed volume. It is from these unpreached sermons that Newman's rhetorical intent can be inferred.

I will adopt the expression "on schedule" to identify sermons written a short time, a week or less, before they were to be preached. All of Volume 2's preached sermons were written on schedule, that is, within a week of being delivered orally. Because the feasts of St. Thomas, St. John the Evangelist and the Holy Innocents fall within December, they were composed on schedule, being "written or first preached" (see dates listed in *Sermons on Subjects of the Day*, 412) on 21 Dec

1834, 27 Dec 1831 and 28 Dec 1833 respectively. So, too, with the sermons for the January feast of St. Paul (sermon dated 25 Jan 1831), the February feasts of the Purification of Mary (2 Feb 1832) and Saint Matthias (24 Feb 1832). The same is true of the April and August feasts of Saints Mark (25 Apr 1831) and Bartholomew (24 Aug 1831). These eight sermons illustrate Newman's habitual procedure, wherein composition shortly before oral delivery is the norm.

The other half of the volume's sermons were written off schedule, i.e., months out of step with the feast days they represent. For example, Newman wrote specifically for Volume 2 two sermons which were composed in "1835, Jan. or Feb." yet designated as intended for the Monday and Tuesday of Easter Week, which falls in late March or April. These two sermons clearly were not written to be preached in St. Mary's Church, not only on account of the uncharacteristic time lag between writing and delivery, but because Newman elsewhere tells us that the church building would have been deserted then ("We dare not open our churches" during "the week-day Festivals and various Holy Seasons" for fear that "men should profane them instead of worshipping" (PS, II, 398–9)). These two sermons, written in the opening days of 1835 but intended for Easter Week, are useful as indicating Newman's intention for Volume 2. So, too, are the sermons for Saints Philip and James, and for the Ascension, both of them May feasts, though their sermons were written in 1834, "December 27" and "end of year" respectively. The three sermons for Pentecost Sunday and for the Monday and Tuesday of Pentecost Week, which occurs in May or June, are dated "1834, end of year" and "1835, Jan. or Feb." Similarly off schedule are the sermons for St. Barnabas and St. Peter, whose festivals occur in June, and the sermons celebrating the July and October feasts of St. James, and Saints Simon and Jude. To sum up the evidence, the on-schedule sermons are intended to fill out the Table of Holy Days framework, while the off-schedule sermons, written just before Newman forwarded his copy to Rivingtons for printing, reveal the thematic intent Newman had in mind immediately prior to dedicating this volume to J. W. Bowden on "Feb 21, 1835."

Now while Newman's authorial intentions in his sermons can be inferred from the sermons themselves, his general state of mind between November, 1834 and February, 1835 is expressed in his contemporary letters to correspondents, particularly those to his one-time mentor Richard Whately, now Archbishop of Dublin, his friend Hurrell Froude, then in Barbados convalescing from the illness that would soon kill him, and James Stephen, an acquaintance irritated by what he thought Newman's bad treatment of the Evangelicals. Whately begins their late-1834 correspondence by writing Newman on 25 October to inquire about "a most shocking report concerning you," i.e., that when the Archbishop visited Oxford earlier in the year "you absented yourself from Chapel on purpose to avoid receiving the Communion along with me" and publicly "declared this to be the case" (L

& D, IV, 348). Newman replies by denying the charge but referring, somewhat angularly and with little detail, to the lack of a common mind between them, stating that, in conversations with his friends, he would vacillate between praise and protest "according as the affectionate remembrances which I had of you rose against my utter aversion to the secular and unbelieving policy" which, as Dublin's Archbishop, Whately has supported in Ireland. His policy decisions "are but the legitimate offspring of those principles, difficult to describe in few words, with which your reputation is especially associated," says Newman (IV, 349). Within a week, Whately fires back his reply, which includes the officious suggestion that "there was plainly nothing to preclude you from offering friendly admonition (when your view of my principles changed) with a full confidence of being at least patiently and kindly listened to" (IV, 357). Still reluctant to pick a fight by going into great detail, though determined to be candid, Newman replies to Whately's suave remonstrance that "the opinions to which I especially alluded in my former letter . . . are those which may be briefly described as the Anti-superstition notions; and to these I do not recollect ever assenting . . . I would instance the under valuing of antiquity, and of resting on one's own reasonings, judgments, definitions etc rather than authority and precedent." As to their former friendship, "it is natural that, when two persons pursue different lines from the same point, they should not discover their divergence for a long while; especially if there be any kind of feeling in the one towards the other. It was not for a very long time that I discovered that your opinions"——the opinions, that is, of an influential Archbishop of the Anglican Church——were "so dangerous" (IV, 358–9).

Newman's pertinent letter to Froude (January 18, 1835) replies to his friend's letter of November 23, written on the one-year anniversary of his sailing from England to the mild climate of Barbados, where his convalescence is going rather badly. "Filled with anxiety" at Froude's inability to recover health, Newman writes to console and encourage him, to keep him abreast of his companions' activities in England and to make small talk, since nothing else will do. "A second volume of sermons is coming out——half through the press," he tells him. Also, "I have seen a good deal of [Hugh] Rose in the last ten days . . . [W]e excogitated the rise of a *judicial* power in the Church." What need of such a power? "The abandonment of State prosecutions for blasphemy etc. and the disordered state of the Christian Knowledge Society when books are taken cognizance of and condemned, make it *desirable* that there should be some (really working) court of heresy and false doctrine." What practical benefits might be associated with such a court?

> The whole Church would be kept in order. Further, it would give rise to a *school of theology*——the *science* of divinity, Councils etc, the *theological law* of the Church must be revived, and ecclesiastical law moreover. The effect of this upon the divinity of the Clergy would be great indeed. At present you hear Nestorianism preached in every other pulpit, etc. etc.

(and the more I think of those questions, the more I feel, that they are questions of *things* not *words*.) Lastly, how to introduce this change?

Unfortunately, neither Newman nor Rose can think of any way to effect such changes: "[t]here's a fine scheme for you which is but an air-castle after all" (V, 9–10). As such correspondence shows, Newman during the time when he is preparing Volume 2 for the press is deeply concerned that the forces of religious dissolution continue to increase unabated in England, and those who might stem the tide are either dying in Barbados or cannot see their way to doing what needs to be done.

Newman's February 27, 1835 letter to James Stephen has its proximate genesis in his February 4 letter to Samuel Wilberforce, which the recipient forwarded to Stephen to read and return to Newman. Stephen returns the letter, adding some obviously irritated remarks, the pertinent one being this: "What I may have said [to Wilberforce], has very nearly escaped my Memory, except that I well recollect the having imputed to you a contempt for that Body in the Church who are usually called 'Evangelical' . . ." (V, 31). In fact, Newman did not feel contempt for the Evangelicals, having in his youth been one of them, and understood further that their position is simply one of the effects of the general denaturing of English Christianity, such that disappointment, concern, and the like would better describe his feelings with respect to the Evangelicals *as people*; their theological position is quite another matter. Newman writes Stephen as follows:

> Nothing I believe in my Sermons is against them except as far as they hold certain opinions, which they hold more or less, some in name, others consistently. Against the *spirit* of their school certainly I have spoken strongly; and, while I believe . . . that that spirit tends to liberalism and Socinianism, I ever must. This is the reason for my strong language, my fear of a system of doctrine which eats out the heart of godliness, where truer and holier instincts do not exclude it from producing its legitimate results. If this be so, it is . . . a matter of duty to hinder (if it be possible) excellent men from what may prove a snare to them, and what on the long run certainly . . . tends to one form or other of infidelity . . . On the other hand I consider that a large portion of the deepest and truest religious principle in the country has been seduced into this corrupt (as I think it) school; and that, for want of deeper views, being authoritatively set forth by the Church. This of course creates mingled feelings, of shame at the Church's neglect, respect for the individuals in question, fear lest they be corrupted by the School which has absorbed them, and grief, perhaps impatience, at the sanction given it by their names. V. 32

Because the same word, "vision," appears both in the book's title and in this chapter's title, it may help avoid confusion if I explain what the word means as used in this chapter. Newman's "vision" of the Church means his idea of it, his conception of it, his distinctive way of seeing it, which should not be confused with the word's different use in "visionary georgic." Newman was a Christian Minister with pastoral duties at a time when the English Church was continuing its long slide into sectarian multiplicity. Expressing that general state of affairs somewhat wryly a decade later, he says that the hypothesis "has met with wide reception in these latter times, that Christianity does not fall within the province of history—that it is to each man what each man thinks it to be, and nothing else" (*Development of Doctrine*, 31–2). Newman can be accurately thought of as a latter-day Saint Paul, whose constant preoccupation is fear of betraying his trust, i.e., woe unto me if I neglect to preach the Gospel. When influential churchmen including Whately, Milman and Hampden contribute to the dissemination of falsehood, when a large part of "the deepest and truest religious principle" in England drifts into error for want of "deeper views, being authoritatively set forth by the Church," it is incumbent upon a Minister who understands his function to respond to the challenge. In this regard, Newman's situation has been aptly described by Aquinas, a pertinent voice because the Christian Minister's situation remains constant over time. Says Aquinas, "when once a Law has been given, it is for a wise man to induce men not only to observe the precepts, but also, and much more, to safeguard the foundation of the Law" (*ST*, II.IIae, 22.2). This is the advice which Newman will in Volume 2 propose to laymen, enlisting their aid in a time of official defection to defend orthodox Christianity, lest the Gospel be lost to generations yet unborn.

Newman's vision of Christian truth is essentially that of the Apostles: it is the unprecedented intervention of God Himself in human affairs, God's taking into Himself our human nature as a permanent facet of His divine nature, thus raising the curtain on the drama that was prophesied in the Old Testament, begun in earnest by the Incarnation, and transferred into human hands for furtherance in time to come by the Holy Spirit's having commissioned the Apostles at Pentecost to begin preaching the Gospel to all nations—a drama which will continue to unfold until the Ascended Son of God returns in glory to judge the nations and bring down the curtain upon the earth by subsuming time into eternity. And yet Newman's "Vision of the Church" includes as well the note of particularity in time and place, the time being his own century, the place being the English Anglican Church and its forms of worship. For Newman, the Christian life is signified and enabled by common worship, especially by the commemoration and renewal of Christ's actions and the Spirit's sanctifying influence as these are embodied in the feasts of the Church calendar, which is the circling repetition, from one revolution of the liturgical calendar to the next, of God's timeless activity among us. It is just this particularity in Newman's conception of the Church that accounts for his adopting the Table of Feast Days as the underlying paradigm of Volume 2, and one is not surprised to discover that the saints' day sermons are less important for the volume's purpose than are the doctrinal sermons.

The purpose of the volume's first doctrinal sermon, "The Incarnation," is to explain the origin of doctrinal statements as the necessary defense against corruptions of the Gospel truth. The sermon consists of three sections, the first describing the genesis and function of Christian dogmas, the second explaining the Incarnation, the third illustrating the ways in which that doctrine has fallen prey to various corruptions, as for example, Nestorianism's claim that there are two distinct persons in Christ, and Socinianism's rejection of Christ's divinity along with the Trinity and original sin. Newman begins the sermon by contrasting the simple faith of the early Christians that, in Christ, God had become man, with the "lawless doubtings, importunate inquirings" and "confident reasonings" that arose when "love waxed cold" and heretics began to alter and unravel what the Apostles had preached. "Such is the difference," Newman points out, "between our own state" of doctrinal confusion "and that of the early church," namely, that carefully written creeds are now necessary to explain misconceptions, allay doubts, and silence innovators. On the other hand, the creeds of the Church offer the positive benefit of preserving Christians "from the indolent use of words without apprehending them." Used in that way, they help to "kindle and elevate the religious affections."

The second section of "The Incarnation" explains the doctrine according to which Christ became Man, taking upon Himself "our imperfections without having any share in our sinfulness," so that He might raise up humanity to intimate fellowship with Himself. Newman dwells on the corporality of Christ's taking our human nature into his divinity, and does so at some length because that is the point upon which heretics always focus their attacks.

> Thus He came, selecting and setting apart for Himself the elements of body and soul; then, uniting them to Himself from their first origin of existence, pervading them, hallowing them by His own Divinity, spiritualizing them, and filling them with light and purity, the while they continued to be human, and for a time mortal and exposed to infirmity. And as they [the elements of body and soul] grew from day to day in their holy union [during the period of gestation in Mary's womb], His Eternal Essence still was one with them, exalting them, acting in them, manifesting Itself through them, so that He was truly God and Man. 2.10

It is as if the Son of God exercised direct and continuing control to ensure the efficacy of His own fetal development up to the moment of the Nativity, beyond which point Newman condenses Christ's earthly life into a single sentence, one with the taut brevity of the Church's creedal statements, of which this sentence is itself one version: "He begun His ministry, preached the Gospel, chose His Apostles, suffered on the cross, died, and was buried, rose again and ascended on high, there to reign till the day when He comes again to judge the world."

The final portion of the sermon reviews some of the Scriptural "modes" whereby God presented Himself on earth, all of them manifestations which fall short of

Christ's Incarnation, all of them modes to which heretics have often attempted to reduce His essential being. Thus for example, they claim that Christ "merely showed Himself as a vision or phantom," or that "the Word of God merely dwelt in the man Christ Jesus," or that "Christ was called God for His great spiritual perfections, and that He gradually attained them by long practice." As the iteration of such falsehood through the ages shows, doctrinal statements are essential, since "when evil men and seducers abound," as Newman found in his own day, "and our own apprehensions of the Truth are dull," which is the case in every place and time, we need creeds to repel enemies and strengthen our faith, as Newman emphatically teaches the readers of Volume 2.

Following "The Incarnation" in the same liturgical season, the Epiphany sermon "The Glory of the Christian Church" examines prophecy, which looks through time to see history before it happens, and providence, which effects God's purposes in spite of the impediments raised by human failure. This sermon as well has a three-part structure, the first of which reflects upon the prophecies that the "door of faith" would open to the Gentiles and thus ensure the "dissemination of the Truth throughout the world." This section is given its focus by the question, "often asked," whether such prophecies have been accomplished or whether "a more complete Christianizing" can be expected. Newman's first response is to caution that the Apostles' mandate to evangelize all nations "for a witness unto" them appears to imply that many will ignore that witness. What, then, are we to expect from evangelization? Says Newman,

> the system of the world depends in a way unknown to us, both on God's Providence and our human agency. Every event, every course of action, has two faces; it is divine and perfect, and it belongs to man and is marked with sin. I observe next, that it is a peculiarity of Holy Scripture to represent the world on its providential side; ascribing all that happens in it to Him who rules and directs it, as it moves along, tracing events to His sole agency, or viewing them only so far forth as He acts in them . . . [It is common] for Scripture to consider Dispensations, not in their actual state but as His agency would mould them, and so far as it really does succeed in moulding them . . . In other words, Scripture more commonly speaks of the Divine *design* and *substantial work*, than of the *measure* of fulfilment which it receives at this time or that. 2.83

The principle is that in His dealings with the world, given the impediment "that man is imperfect, and has a will of his own, and lives in time, and is moved by circumstances," God appears to work "by a process, by means and ends, by steps," winning here, losing there, but at last governing the outcome. Scripture, as Newman says, "anticipating the end from the beginning," presents the outcome at the outset, as, for instance, in the history of Abraham, who "trusted in God's power to raise the dead," and in that belief was afforded "a vision of the Atoning Sacrifice on Calvary" long before Pilate sent Christ to the cross. Thus Scripture pictures God revealing events which will in time occur, yet which are but "gradually unfolded to our limited faculties, and in this transitory scene."

Applying this principle of deferred fulfilment, Newman explains that the Church "had in the day of its nativity" all that it was ever to have, but that that fulfilment is "viewed as God's work in its tendency," as picturing "what it will be absolutely in heaven." That is to say, promises given to the Church shall be fulfilled "only in the course of its history, as foreshortened and viewed as one whole." The obvious corollary is that we cannot at any given moment grasp the current state of prophecy's fulfilment. And yet the glory momentarily revealed at Christ's Transfiguration "is a token held out to us in our dark age, that His promise stands sure, and admits of accomplishment." The brief concluding section of the sermon instructs readers that hungering after signs and wonders runs counter to the spirit of the Gospel, which adjures us to rely upon God's promises, and to "enjoy the fruit of them" even before they are fulfilled. What is this, after all, but the faith of Abraham? Bringing this advice closer to home (the England of Whatley, Milman and Hampden), while doing what we can to advance God's kingdom, "we will not reckon on any visible fruit of our labour" but will rest content "to believe our cause triumphant, when we see it apparently defeated," the while seeking within ourselves for the eventual Epiphany of Christ.

The Easter sermon "Christ, A Quickening Spirit" serves as a doctrinal link between "The Incarnation" (which tells us "corruption had no power over that Sacred Body," formed by a "miraculous conception") and the Pentecost sermon "The Indwelling Spirit." The adjectives tell the story, for the "quickening" of the resurrection is succeeded by the Holy Ghost's "indwelling." This Easter sermon has the additional benefit that it provides Newman two open slots, endorsed by the Table of Holy Days, into which he can insert a pair of sermons on any subject of his choosing, so long as they are generally appropriate for the Monday and Tuesday of Easter week. He uses the opportunity to advance his investigation of true and false doctrines by describing right and wrong *attitudes* towards them, in the only two doctrinal sermons of the volume exclusively devoted to personal conduct.

The epigraph "Why seek ye the living among the dead?" extends its reference in this sermon from its primary meaning, the risen Christ's absence from the empty tomb, to its secondary application for Christian believers, as an earnest of "their own Resurrection unto glory" as well as "His Divine Power to conduct them safely to it." It is as if, just as Adam's sin was infectious, Christ's quickening power too reaches beyond Himself, raising the mass of his followers, as yeast leavens dough wherein it is introduced, by intimate contact. Indeed, with regard to such intimacy, Newman advances from Christ's resurrection to the "special mode of approaching Him" which the Church provides, namely, the Eucharist, in which by "feasting upon the Sacrifice," we become partakers of His divine nature. When we receive the Eucharist, we are filled with "a spiritual life which may expel the poison of the tree of knowledge." On the other hand, those who disregard the Eucharist may, "as time goes on," learn "deliberately to doubt" that it is a real source of grace. Is it wonderful that such a person

> should no longer look upon . . . the Lord's Minister who consecrates it as a chosen vessel, or that Holy Church in which he ministers as a Divine Ordinance, to be cherished as a parting legacy of Christ to a sinful world? Is it wonderful that seeing he sees not . . . and that, lightly regarding all the gifts of Christ, he feels no reverence for the treasure-house wherein they are stored? 2.149

Though Easter is a joyful feast, Newman moderates the high emotion appropriate to the time by briefly reflecting upon the doctrinal disintegration which Volume 2 is intended to counteract, saying "in this time of rebuke and blasphemy, we cannot but be sober and subdued in our rejoicing."

"Saving Knowledge" and "Self-Contemplation," for the Monday and Tuesday of Easter week, compare a sound approach to the Gospel against a mischievous, because self-absorbed, attitude. Unlike the Heathens' blind faith, which gropes its way "in the darkness," the faith of Christians is a genuine form of knowledge, one that permits us to see "the invisible God" and contemplate "the history of His sojourn" among us. Nevertheless, it is possible to mistake "some dream of our own" for the Gospel truth, and these two sermons investigate how we can distinguish "the true and clear Vision" from imaginary constructions of our own making. The test of sincerity, says Newman, is obedience, i.e., doing God's will, for faith and obedience are the Christian's whole duty. Yet this truth has become obscured for some.

> I conceive that we are in danger, in this day, of insisting on neither of these as we ought; regarding all true and careful consideration of the Object of faith, as barren orthodoxy, technical sublety, and the like, and all due earnestness about good works as a mere cold and formal morality; and, instead, making religion, or rather (for this is the point) making the test of our being religious, to consist in our having what is called a spiritual state of heart, to the comparative neglect of the Object from which it must arise, and the works in which it should issue. 2.154

The best means of defense against the corruption of divine truth are the Church's creeds and expositions of doctrine. These "speak of no ideal being, such as the imagination alone contemplates," but of the Son of God, whose actions are recorded in the Gospels. Unfortunately, the incipient heretic objects to this view, insisting that the Christian must "search himself, examine his motives" for evidence that his heart is right, since all the faith and obedience in the world are pointless unless the heart is pure. The problem, says Newman, is that no standard of the heart's purity can be found: how can a person "duly examine his feelings and affections by the light within him?" Here we can see the Cambridge Platonists' candle of the Lord still glowing bright in the nineteenth century, still leading the unwary Christian towards febrile solipsism. The better procedure is to "go out of" ourselves in order to "assay and ascertain" the principles that determine our thinking.

This first sermon of the matched set is the obverse of "Self-Contemplation," which examines in much greater detail the religious error that has already been described by its companion. Here, at the center of Volume 2, we encounter its most sustained and powerful exposure of the dangerous mistake of substituting self-contemplation for faith and obedience. How, asks Newman, does "the fashion of the day" conceive of faith? For persons of that persuasion, it is the central message of the Gospel, which in itself is true enough, but for them the test that one lives by faith is "to insist upon no doctrine but it." Dividing faith into two kinds, living and dead, they insist that the truth may be held "in a carnal and unrenewed mind," which means that one lacks "real feelings and convictions." Against this view, Newman raises the skeptical question concerning their "living" faith, i.e., "whether such frames of mind as *are* directly ascertainable and profess to be spiritual, are not rather a delusion, a mere excitement, capricious feeling, fanatic fancy, and the like." To anchor one's beliefs upon the contemplation of a putative light within the mind is to "obliterate" the truths of the Gospel, to "darken" the eye of faith, and effectively "throw us back into the vagueness of Heathenism," a time "when men only felt after the Divine Presence."

Such wrong notions of faith are typically accompanied by an undervaluing of the need for obedience such as would be demonstrated by good works. It is clear that the system in question is unevangelical; it is so with respect to "the inspired documents" of Christianity, the doctrines they bring to light, the "Sacramental Institutions which are the gift of it," and the theology which interprets it. Setting aside these foundations of genuine Christianity, the system being described relies upon "a continual self-contemplation and reference to self, in all departments of conduct." These views, when fully activated, lead those who hold them progressively further from the vision of Christ seen by the eye of faith. Sounding remarkably like Samuel Johnson in his *Rambler* essay mode, Newman observes that

> He who has learned to give names to his thoughts and deeds, to appraise them as if for the market, to attach to each its due measure of commendation or usefulness, will soon involuntarily corrupt his motives by pride or selfishness. A sort of self-approbation will insinuate itself into his mind: so subtle as not at once to be recognized by himself,—an habitual quiet self-esteem, leading him to prefer his own views to those of others, and a secret, if not avowed persuasion, that he is in a different state from . . . those around him. 2.171

This evil is often associated with religious journals, the danger being that persons who record their subjectivity find great difficulty in "banishing the thought that one day these good feelings will be known to the world," for "seldom indeed is any one in the *practice* of contemplating his better thoughts or doings without displaying them to others." If an aside be permitted here, such a person is on the way to seeing the candle of the Lord shining through the pages of the romantic poet, who brings to the world the Good News perceived by the Spirit of the Age. Concluding the sermon, Newman, in his role as Visionary Georgicist, says "we have seen the effects of them [such self-regarding principles] two centuries since in the history of the English Branch of the Church; for what we know, a more fearful triumph is still in store for them." Yet for all that, "let not the watchmen of Jerusalem fail to give timely warning of the approaching enemy, or to acquit themselves of all cowardice or compliance as regards it."

The important words in the sermon titles "Christ, A Quickening Spirit" and "The Indwelling Spirit" are the two adjectives, of course, but even more so the noun which they modify, spirit, which signifies a supernatural, incorporeal being that is by definition neither visible nor tangible. Therein lies the difficulty which Newman addresses in his Pentecost sermon "The Indwelling Spirit," namely, that neither the ascended Christ nor the Holy Ghost come within our natural perceptions, whereas, to the contrary, the productions, the reflections, insights and waking visions of our own minds have a quasi-visual quality, a density and a graspable presence which testifies to their reality, their force, and in that sense their truth. As Newman has expressed it in "Self-Contemplation," it is possible to "give names" to one's thoughts and thereby exercise a kind of dominion and ownership over them. One can "appraise them as if for the market" and take pride in that self-generated flock of insights, the sheep of one's pasture, the source and guarantor of the "habitual quiet self-esteem" which persuades a person "to prefer his own views" over those of others, including the Church which Christ established to announce and protect his saving truths.

Now while the productions of the human mind are much the most interesting phenomena in the world, their only competitor being the wonders of the earth and universe which the mind explores and comes to understand, Christ's and the Holy Spirit's mission in the world is to remake our being by transforming the natural man into a creature capable of living in the presence of God. The epigraph of "The Indwelling Spirit" is St. Paul's remark to the Romans, "Ye are not in the flesh, but in the Spirit, if so be that the Spirit of God dwell in you" (viii.9). Such a reshaping spirit-possession of the natural man's attitudes, insights and desires is, says Newman, "incomprehensible," since it is not only an invisible operation but one that is beyond the grasp of reason. And yet, because it is the heart of Christianity, the Christian Minister is obliged to take up the difficult task of explaining and clarifying it. Newman begins that effort in this sermon by distinguishing between Christ's external communication of God's truth, and the Spirit's interior workings. The sermon begins by stating that contrast: "God the Son has graciously vouchsafed to reveal the Father to His creatures from without; God the Holy Ghost by inward communications." That distinction being essential, the sermon will necessarily discuss the Trinity, all three persons of the triune God—-Christ's revelation of the Father "from without" during his sojourn on earth being followed by the Spirit's "inward" revelation of the Father. This discussion of the inter-relationships within the Trinity is thematically linked with the earlier sermon "Self-Contemplation," for the self-communication of the heretic—-his own Shepherd, exploring the pasture-land of reason and celebrating the independent competence of his own thought—-sets him going on a collision course with the equally inward though impalpable action of the Holy Ghost. Thus the argument that Newman has already initiated will be continued here, on the same "inward" front, but by taking a different tack.

Comparing their complementary functions, Newman describes Christ as "that Image of God's unapproachable Attributes, which men have ever seen by glimpses on the face of the world," i.e., those signs of divinity which the Heathen groped after in the dark. Equally, the Holy Spirit "has ever been the secret Presence of God within the Creation," bringing order and life to what had been without form and void. But beyond that, and more important for us, the Spirit is the voice of conscience, "the voice of Truth in the hearts of all rational beings, tuning them into harmony with the intimations of God's Law, which were externally made to them." The metaphor of tuning a musical instrument is just right for Newman's meaning, because rational insight is not the origin of self-deceiving error if it be properly tuned. However, the mind cannot perform the tuning operation upon itself without the intervention of the divine tuner, "if so be that the Spirit of God dwell in you." The Holy Spirit, once "the inward light" of the patriarchs, is now both "the Grace abiding in the Christian soul, and the Lord and Ruler of the Church." Here one sees the close connection between the soul and the Church, the "Grace abiding" in the former deriving from the latter, the Church, which has no function except to be the instrument and vehicle of its Lord and Ruler.

The important distinction Newman now makes is that between a merely figurative indwelling, and the Spirit's literal presence in and operations on the Christian's soul, "by a real not a figurative indwelling." Newman explains the Spirit's indwelling with such persistence because it is his Ministerial duty not to passively allow his auditors to use words indolently "without apprehending them" but rather to "kindle and elevate" their religious affections. If the doctrine of the Holy Ghost's indwelling is difficult, and thus easily sloughed off and discarded, the more the need to give sustained focal attention to its importance.

Continuing his explication, Newman says that the Holy Ghost comes to us as Christ came, "by a real and personal visitation," first as the itinerant preacher in

Palestine, then as the invisible power the Christian receives in the Eucharist. Departing this world, Christ left "His Spirit for Himself, and that, both in the Church and in the souls of individual Christians." In other words, the business of the Church is spirit possession, its role being to enable the Holy Ghost to live within those who cooperate with the Church's divine mission. The consequent operation of the Holy Spirit brings the Christian into "a state altogether new and marvellous" (St. Peter), one in which he is given the power "to become the son of God" (St. John) and "a new creation" (St. Paul). Here, Newman ends the first portion of the sermon, the half which explains how the "manifold benefits" of Christ's blood are applied to us individually. Newman describes this as a "great doctrine, which we hold as a matter of faith, and without actual experience to verify it to us." Do we grope forward in the dark like the Heathen? No, for we see by the eye of faith, taking God's Word in the place of "actual experience." Once again, we meet the radical difference separating those who trust in self-contemplation from those who rely upon Revelation.

The second half of the sermon undertakes an equally difficult task, since it attempts to explain how the Holy Ghost's gift of Grace "manifests itself in the regenerate soul." This is a subject, says Newman,

> which I do not willingly take up, and which no Christian perhaps is ever able to consider without some effort, feeling that he thereby endangers either his reverence towards God, or his humility, but which the errors of this day, and the confident tone of their advocates, oblige us to dwell upon, lest truth should suffer by our silence. 2.224

Thus we recognize at mid-sermon the restatement of Newman's purpose in Volume 2, the theme we infer from the sermons he wrote during the three-month period before submitting his copy to Rivingtons for printing; that theme is the need to counter the doctrinal degeneration of the English Church. Now the attempt to investigate the manifestations "in the regenerate soul," of a spiritual transformation that Newman admits is incomprehensible, one which offers us no "actual experience to verify it," puts the writer to the difficult test of finding an adequate language to meet the task. For all their great differences, Newman and Wordsworth shared that difficulty. At his best, Wordsworth succeeds quite well in finding an adequate language to express realities which the mother tongue seldom tries to articulate, as in his lines "Fallings from us, vanishings;/ Blank misgivings of a Creature/ Moving about in worlds not realized" ("Ode: Intimations of Immortality . . . ," 143–45), which nicely expresses the experience of dimly perceiving the nature of a mystery which impinges upon and fascinates, but cannot be brought fully to light and adequately explained.

Since Newman's subject is the Holy Ghost's indwelling, a truth which is held upon faith rather than supported by personal experience, he cannot mount an argument based upon the testimony of personal intuitions, as does Wordsworth. He proceeds by dividing his presentation into three sub-sections, each of them specifying one of the "manners in which" the Holy Ghost's presence "manifests itself." Its first manifestation is that it "fixes the eyes of our mind" upon God the Father, in whose Image we were created, a mode of being we lost after Adam fell, and by thus fixing our mind's eye, the Spirit "disposes us to seek His presence by the very instinct of our new nature." It turns our mind "towards Him, rather than thinking of ourselves," thus making God's Will and Kingdom the great realities for the Christian to "contemplate and make his portion." Having dismissed one's own experience as verifying the Spirit's presence, Newman appears to contradict himself by offering his own experience as verification, for he explains that if the Christian has, in time of suffering or trial,

> special visitations and comfortings from the Spirit, "plaints unutterable" within him, yearnings after the life to come, or bright and passing gleams of God's eternal election, and deep stirrings of wonder and thankfulness thence following, he thinks too reverently of "the secret of the Lord," to betray (as it were) His confidence, and, by vaunting it to the world, to exaggerate it perchance into more than it was meant to convey: but he is silent, and ponders it as choice encouragement to his soul, meaning something, but he knows not how much. 2.226

A second effect of the Holy Ghost's indwelling is to raise the soul "not only to the thought of God, but of Christ also," for the Spirit came to "glorify" Christ, and towards that end "vouchsafes to be a shining light within" the Church and the individual Christian, "reflecting the Saviour of the World in all His perfections, all His offices, all His works." Thus, for instance, the Spirit inspired the evangelists to record Christ's life, thereby making "history to be doctrine." As the Church developed, the Spirit guided and governed its "human instruments," making Christ's actions and the Apostles' illustrations of them into "permanent ordinances." The Spirit completed His work by then "conveying this system of truth, thus varied and expanded," into the hearts of believers. It is no coincidence that this sermon was composed in "1834, end of year," and that in November Dr. Hampden, soon to become the head of Oxford's theological teaching, mailed Newman a copy of his *Observations on Religious Dissent.* Nor is it surprising that Newman replied by accusing Hampden that his principles tend "altogether to make shipwreck of Christian faith," because his *Observations* assert that "Religion is distinct from Theological Opinion," that such theological opinion included both Trinitarian and Unitarian doctrines, that dogma was theological opinion formally insisted upon, and that the Church of England "was not dogmatic in its spirit, though the wording of its formularies might often carry the sound of dogmatism" (Newman, *Apologia,* 73–4). A third manifestation of the Holy Spirit's operative presence in particular Christians is peace, the absence of anxiety over one's state of soul. That is, the Spirit's indwelling releases the believer from "the dread, which the natural man feels, of an offended, unreconciled Creator." In this sermon, Newman presents the ideal which Christians ought to aim at, for he has described "not so much what we have" as what we should have.

Newman is a Visionary Georgicist not in the sense that he discovered new truths but that he valued old ones, and therefore he opposed the revisionists who, embarrassed by the supernatural, either suppressed or ignored it. Though a scandal to rationalizing churchmen, Mystery, Miracle and Prophecy are the bedrock realities that Newman defended and preached. "The Glory of the Christian Church" expresses his conviction that divine Providence is not a mere figure but an effective Power overcoming human opposition—that being humanity's role in the drama which has been gathering momentum ever since the Incarnation. "The Kingdom of the Saints" supplements the earlier sermon by demonstrating that Prophecy, which unerringly reveals God's intention, became history in the early spread of Christianity. "The Kingdom of the Saints" is a single extended argument which Newman has for convenience broken into two sermons which share the same title and epigraph, which he designated as appropriate for the Monday and Tuesday of Pentecost week. That placement in Volume 2 is appropriate because the Holy Spirit's effect of energizing the Apostles to go forth and preach the Gospel changed the course of history, as was prophesied by Daniel when he stated that "The stone that smote the Image became a great Mountain, and filled the earth" (2:35). "The Kingdom of the Saints" addresses both God's effecting the diffusion of Christianity into the whole world, and, in keeping with this volume's theme, the limitations imposed upon that success by human failures.

If we could see "the course of God's dispensations in this world" as do the angels, and along with them the saints in the Apocalypse who cry out "Great and marvellous are thy works, Lord God Almighty," we could neither deny nor be in doubt, says Newman, that "His unseen hand" had ordered them. Yet despite our inability to see God's works from the perspective of eternity, "even to us" is given "some insight into God's providence, by means of the records of it," i.e., history and Prophecy. The history of Christianity's spread throughout the world lies before us, while the other "record" of that event is Daniel's prophecy that "In the days of these kings shall the God of heaven set up a kingdom, which shall never be destroyed" (2:44). Rising to the lyrical opportunity afforded by this divine operation, Newman reflects on the fact that, in the midst of the great Roman Empire, "suddenly a new kingdom arose."

> [I]n the East and West, North and South, as if by some general understanding, yet without
> any sufficient correspondence or centre of influence, ten thousand orderly societies, pro-
> fessing one and the same doctrine, and disciplined upon the same polity, sprang up as from

the earth. It seemed as though the fountains of the great deep were broken up, and some new forms of creation were thrown forward from below, the manifold ridges of some "great Mountain," crossing, splitting, disarranging the existing system of things, levelling the hills, filling up the valleys,—irresistible as being sudden, unforeseen, and unprovided for,—till it "filled the whole earth" [Isaiah 41: 15–16]. This was indeed a "new thing;" and independent of all reference to prophecy, is unprecedented in the history of the world before or since, and calculated to excite the deepest interest and amazement in any really philosophical mind. 2.377

Everywhere in his dominion the Roman emperor would find the Bishops of the Church, who traced their religion back to "certain twelve or fourteen Jews, who professed to have received it from Heaven." When the civil power gradually declined, the bishops became the empire's "patrons instead of its enemies," mediating between it and its barbarian enemies. The most striking concomitant of this sudden appearance and widespread dissemination of the Church is the placid conviction of its first adherents that this new kingdom would grow and triumph. They "speak confidently," even while being "tossed to and fro as outcasts among the heathen," and do so even while admitting the inevitability of what Newman calls "those miserable corruptions in the Church, which all Christians allow to have since taken place," because of those false prophets whose corruptions of the truth will "deceive the very elect."

The Monday installment of "The Kingdom of the Saints" having covered the Church's broad extention and "unlimited duration," along with the "boldness and correctness" of the Apostles in foreseeing that outcome, the Tuesday sermon completes Newman's exposition by making two further points. First, both in the Old Testament and in Simeon's prophecy during Christ's presentation in the temple, one finds the same linkage between "bloody revolution" and "peace," since God's Kingdom is "at once a refuge and consolation, and a sword." This aspect of prophecy had its fulfilment, says Newman, in the "wars and tumults" of the medieval period, of which the Church "was the occasion." His second point is that the state of the Jews during the four centuries before Christ was God's preparation for what was to follow, as the wanderings of Abraham and his heirs, their descent into Egypt and lengthy captivity there had prepared for the establishment of the Jewish Church. What was the nature of God's remote preparation for the spread of Christianity?

The overthrow of the nation by the Chaldeans, issued in the dispersion of its members all over the civilized world, so that in all the principal cities Jewish communities existed, which . . . attracted to their faith Gentile converts, and were in one way or other the nucleus of the Christian Church when the Gospel was at length published. 2.250

Returning to the thematic preoccupation of Volume 2, Newman once more discusses the interference with Providence caused by human opposition to the divine will. Although he does not say that the case of the Papacy "parallels" that of the

Jewish monarchy, he does say that "the Latin ecclesiastical system of the Middle Ages" was in essence the fulfilment of God's design, but that its fulfilment "would have been even more exactly accomplished" had Christians not strayed from His express will. "Had it not been for this falling away in divers times and places, surely Christendom would not be in its present miserable state of disunion and feebleness." Nor is the English Church exempt from such criticism. "As for ourselves, what was the exact measure of the offences of our forefathers in the faith, when they tired of the Christian theocracy, and clothed the Church with 'the purple robe' of Caesar, it avails not to determine." Here, Newman is accusing the British civil authority, but doing that so indirectly that the charge of religious malfeasance is muted and loses its sting by becoming generic. So does his lamentation that the English are "the sinful offspring of sinful parents," which can as well refer to Adam and Eve as to the English reformers of earlier centuries. Thus the pattern in which human failure infects the work of divine providence is the focus of Newman's criticism, rather than the assigning of blame for Christianity's condition to any particular group of Christians during its history.

While it is ostensibly a Trinity Sunday sermon, "The Gospel, A Trust Committed to Us" does not investigate the doctrine of the Trinity, which has already been adequately discussed by "The Indwelling Spirit." Instead, it looks back upon the volume's progression through the Incarnation, the Resurrection and Pentecost, and forward to focus its attention entirely upon the need to "hold fast the form of sound words" (*Timothy*, 2:13). This holding fast to the Church's formulation of Gospel truths requires a sustained effort since the normal human impulse is to be dissatisfied with explanations that one cannot wholly understand, and consequently to seek to explain and clarify what remains mysterious or has no obvious practical utility. Hence, the phenomenon that St. Paul, in the epigraph, warns Timothy to avoid and resist, i.e., the "profane and vain babblings" of contemporary revisionists. The phenomenon continues in the Christian teachers of Newman's day "giving new meanings, modifying received ones," without any bad intention, indeed with "the idea of the True Faith in their minds," relying, however, on their natural powers, with the result that they "embrace a deceit of their own instead of it." Newman in this sermon solicits his audience's aid to defend the Gospel's true sense, because "we have all an equal interest in" preserving it.

The sermon is constructed as a contrast between two opposing investigations, the first undertaken by those who, instead of "accepting reverently" the doctrinal truths the Church is entrusted to protect, "simplify" and "refashion" them into a more palatable form, the second investigation undertaken by such as "in the course of Scripture narrative and precept" can recognize the evident outlines of Church doctrines. Regarding the former, Newman describes it as the "fashion of the day" to think that "all insisting upon precise Articles of Faith" is harmful to the cause of genuine spiritual religion. Thus the fashionable teacher of Christianity "asks himself"

> what is the *use* of the message which has come down to him? . . . He proceeds to assume
> that there is some one end of his ministerial labours . . . Then, perhaps, he arbitrarily assigns
> this end to be the salvation of the world, or the conversion of sinners. Next he measures
> all the Scripture doctrines by their respective sensible tendency to effect this end. He goes
> on to discard or degrade this or that sacred truth as superfluous in consequence, or of inferior importance. 2.260

Sometimes these ministers of the Word convince themselves that theological doctrines are "altogether unnecessary," which is the reason why "you may hear them ask, 'What is the *harm* of being a Sabellian, or Arian? how does it affect the moral character?'" Newman thus dramatizes the process whereby theologically blind teachers wander from the truth.

The sermon shifts then to the contrary investigation, in which "the very text of Scripture" provides one with the "elementary lines" of truth which are further elaborated in the Church's doctrinal forms. Newman gives three reasons why his readers are obligated to uphold orthodox doctrines. First, we have been told to do so, but the difficulty lies in persuading them that "we *have* a trust, a treasure to transmit, for the safety of which they are answerable." Second, the seriousness of that mandate is increased by the fact that we do not know "what is the real final object" of the Gospel's revelation. While we are told that its object is the glory of God, "we cannot understand what is meant by this, or how the Dispensation of the Gospel promotes it." Moreover, we know that "His glory is set forth in some mysterious way" not only in its acceptance, but in the Gospel's rejection as well, "and we must co-operate with Him" even when doing so requires us "to wound as well as heal, to condemn as well as absolve." Newman pursues this line of thought in order to answer those who would limit Christian truth "to what is influential and convincing in it," when we are "utterly in the dark" on the subject and can but "hold fast our treasure and not betray our trust." Yet this is what "wilful and feverish minds" cannot do, for they are bent upon rousing the emotions in the hope of "changing the character," instead of being humble "sowers of that heavenly seed, which He shall make spring up in the hearer's heart to life eternal." Third, we must fulfil our charge because of the divine sanction that whoever does not believe will be damned. In summation, Newman says that we know some doctrines have to be believed, but not how many, "and we have no powers of mind adequate to the task of solving the problem." We cannot give any reason except for the revealed word why the doctrine of the Trinity should be essential, and if not that doctrine, why any other one? It behoves us, therefore, not to "trifle with any portion of the message committed to us."

Newman's brief reminder in "The Gospel, A Trust Committed to Us" that the Christian must cooperate with God even when doing so obliges him "to wound as well as heal" is further elaborated in the last two sermons this chapter will discuss, "Tolerance of Religious Error" and "Christian Zeal." All three were composed at the same moment in time, "1834, end of year," and all three discuss the need for English Christians to overcome their habitual impulse to be pleasant at all costs and say nothing rather than offend. "Tolerance of Religious Error," for the feast of St. Barnabas, celebrates this Apostle's admirable traits, he being a person of "kindness, gentleness, considerateness, warmth of heart, compassion, and munificence." Yet the Christian character requires a full panoply of virtues, and any virtue is a mean between opposing extremes. As Newman points out, St. Barnabas was imperfect in this respect on account of his "indulgence towards the faults of others," whether in matters of doctrine or of conduct, and therefore his example teaches us to take the narrow path between the contrary errors which lie to either side.

The reason why Newman uses this saint's feast day to discuss his characteristic weakness is that St. Barnabas has much in common with the English: "he may be considered as the type of the better sort of men among us, and those who are in most esteem." Generalizing, he observes that in every age the world "chooses some one or other peculiarity of the Gospel as the badge of its particular fashion for the time being, and sets up as objects of admiration those who eminently possess it." Like St. Barnabas, the English are "considerate, delicate" and "courteous" in their social conduct, they are generous to those in need, "the stranger, the fatherless, and the widow." On the other hand, "[w]e are deficient in jealous custody of the revealed Truths which Christ has left us. We allow men to speak against the Church, its ordinances, or its teaching, without remonstrating with them." Popularity is always in fashion because it "excites a glow of pleasure" and self-approval in the person who is well liked, yet the desire to make others happy can harm them, especially if one is

> led on to give up Gospel Truths, to consent to open the Church to the various denominations of error which abound among us, or to alter our Services so as to please the scoffer, the lukewarm, or the vicious. 2.406

Newman presents St. John as the Apostle who strikes the best balance between the opposing vices of too-much and too-little generosity, for he "loved the world so wisely, that he preached the Truth in it," yet if men rejected it, "he did not love them so inordinately as to forget the supremacy of the Truth, as the Word of Him who is above all." Therefore, one must never shrink from proclaiming God's wrath "as a real characteristic of His glorious nature."

"Christian Zeal" celebrates the double feast of those most zealous of Apostles, Simon and Jude. In this sermon Newman moderates the emphasis of "Tolerance of Religious Error" by exploring the opposite vice, i.e., the fierce, harsh defense of God's Truth which can disguise a self-aggrandizing spirit in the defender. St. Jude's epistle opens with the exhortation to "contend earnestly for the faith," which is excellent advice because the principle of all religious service is love of God above everything else, "above our dearest and most intimate friends" if it comes to that. Christ, our model of conduct, manifested himself early in His career by "two acts of Zeal" which slighted or offended others, distressing His mother and St. Joseph by tending to His Father's business as a twelve year old, and driving the money changers out of the Temple because His Father's house ought to be a house of prayer. Thus, zeal is recommended on the highest authority.

But times change, and fashions change with them, and in Newman's day it had become the fashion "to call Zeal by the name of intolerance," and to consider it "the chief of sins." Thus, "any earnestness for one opinion over others concerning God's nature, will, and dealings with man," any action aimed at protecting ortho- dox doctrine, is considered ill-mannered and offensive. Yet on the other hand, zeal is "an imperfect virtue," one that "will ever be attended with unchristian feelings, if it be cherished by itself." Here, Faith steps in and guides us in selecting the cor- rect means along with the correct ends. Zeal's tendency towards self-will—as in Peter's reaction to his "sudden and strong emotion," drawing his sword and strik- ing off the ear of the high priest's servant—needs to be tempered by patience and resignation to God's Will. This is a heavenly corrective which can rein in excess- es, without which zeal begins to expect, and even demand, "results of this world." That misdirection is a serious error in Faith, for God's kingdom is not of this world, as Christ told Pilate, "else would His servants fight." His servants must remember that "the Mystery of Iniquity is to continue till the Avenger solves it once for all." In a nutshell, zeal is ours but vengeance is His. The expectation of achiev- ing "essential improvements" in the conditions of this world will create disappoint- ment in anyone who expects them. As Newman says, "Christian Zeal is not political."

CHAPTER 3

The Persistence
of Divine Allegiance

Divine allegiance points in either of two directions. It refers to God's untiring efforts to ensure the salvation of those who cooperate with Him, and with equal aptness to the individual person's efforts to so cooperate. While it is true that all volumes of *Parochial Sermons* share the same georgic purpose of fostering commitment to Christ and His Church, Volume 3 is particularly well characterized by "divine allegiance" since so many of its sermons focus not on religious doctrine or practical advice, but on the bonds of affection between God and His people.

Though Newman does not say so, the scriptural analogue most germane for this volume is the *Epistle to the Hebrews*, because they share the same concentration upon the divine outreach to humanity and our response, "For both he that sanctifieth and they who are sanctified are all of one: for which cause he is not ashamed to call them brethren" (1:11). In this transaction the divine choice singled us out for particular consideration, "For verily he took not on him the nature of angels; but he took on him the seed of Abraham" (1:16). Further, the Incarnation was specifically intended to bridge the distance between the Creator and His human creatures by enabling them to achieve righteousness, "For in that he himself hath suffered being tempted, he is able to succor them that are tempted" (1:18). Although Newman does not draw attention to it, this relationship is not new to Abraham's seed, for, as *Hebrews* tells us, it has already produced a shining record of achievement in those who overcame difficulty and prevailed in the good fight, such as Abel, Noah, Abraham himself, Jacob, Joseph, Moses, and the harlot Rahab, she who "perished not with those who believed not." Many like them "out of weakness were made strong, waxed valiant in fight," and "stopped the mouths of lions." With that family history behind us, we should be emboldened to "lift up the hands which hang down, and the feeble knees" (12:12), to "run with patience the race that is set before us" (12:1).

But although that is the volume's overall direction, it opens with a sequence of five sermons which in the main highlight the Israelites' failure to remain faithful. These sermons articulate the pattern of defection that Newman finds exemplified in his English contemporaries as well, the same preference for worldly aims covertly undermining allegiance to God's will in both cases. In the first of these, "Abraham and Lot," Newman is so eager to apply Lot's cautionary example to the English that he is less than accurate in his analysis of Lot's conduct. He tells us that "Lot, as well as Abraham, left his own country 'by faith,' in obedience to God's command," but no evidence supports that claim because the *Genesis* narrative attributes to Lot no personal motive whatsoever for his leaving Ur, and even the finest hortatory intent cannot authorize whole cloth invention. We recognize "by faith" as the leitmotif expression in the *Epistle to the Hebrews*' litany of Old Testament heroes, but not only is Lot missing from their number, he never aspired to religious excellence nor raised his sight to anything beyond day-to-day living. *Genesis* all but tells us he was temperamentally incapable of it. What prompted Newman to so misread Lot's character when he reveals himself to be so shrewdly understanding of human nature elsewhere? Obviously, it was the desire to heighten the contrast between Abraham and his nephew, which surely does exist, to make it tell more powerfully against those English Christians "who are religious to a certain point," but are "inconsistent, . . . not aiming at perfection." Newman heightens the scriptural contrast between Lot and his uncle by misattributing to him at the outset a high religious motive, in order later on to charge him with defection from that ideal.

To understand Lot's situation, and therefore the development of his unassertively dependent character, one must examine the narrative which provides the pertinent information. The story of the family's move into Canaan begins with its patriarch, Terah, who had three sons, Abram (listed first and thus the eldest, destined and trained for leadership), Nahor (who disappears after being named), and Haran, the youngest, who, having fathered Lot, prematurely dies, leaving his son the responsibility of his relatives. Lot is in no way a person destined for importance in the family. No one asks his opinions about things, which is the best training for never learning to formulate them. The cast of characters having been provided, the narrative moves into action at the end of Chapter 11: "Terah took Abram his son, and Lot the son of Haran his son's son, and Sarai his daughter in law, . . . and they went forth with them from Ur of the chaldees, to go unto the land of Canaan; and they came unto Haran [a city with the same name as Terah's third son, located about half of the distance to Canaan from Ur], and dwelt there." Now because people do things for reasons and their reasons are stated or implied by the narratives in which they appear, we have to ask why Terah, the patriarch, settled and respected in Ur, would be willing or eager to travel with much bag and baggage toward a strange land a considerable distance away.

No reason is given for Terah's relocation, but one can infer from the beginning of *Genesis*, Chapter 12, that he was persuaded so to act by his eldest son, information that has been suppressed by a narrative stressing Abram's new beginning, leaving his past behind him as it were. This is how the twelfth chapter opens, the patriarch Terah having died in Haran.

> Now the LORD had said unto Abram, Get thee out of thy country, and from thy kindred, and from thy father's house, unto a land that I will shew thee: And I will make thee a great nation . . . So Abram departed, as the LORD had spoken unto him: and Lot went with him: and Abram was seventy and five years old when he departed out of Haran. And Abram took Sarai his wife, and Lot his brother's son, and all their substance that they had gathered in Haran; and they went forth to go unto the land of Canaan; and into the land of Canaan they came. 12: 1–5

The verb tenses—-"had said" and "had spoken"—-locate the Lord's command to move into Canaan at some indefinite point back in time, so that Terah's relocation from Ur to Haran could well have been the first leg of a journey, inspired by God through his messenger Abram, that would eventually bring the family into Canaan. To be sure, the narrative which thus interpreted provides the motivation for Terah to leave Ur poses problems of another sort: how is Abram going "from [his] father's house, and from [his] kindred" if he takes his father and kindred along with him? These are not insuperable problems, though, for the point of the journey-to-Canaan narrative as a whole is that Abram, by whatever means and however accompanied, follows God's command to relocate into Canaan, where, God tells him, "I will make of thee a great nation." Becoming a great nation will never happen unless Abram has the family seed-stock he needs, for one cannot base a great nation upon an airy vision in one's head. Abram will require a son, and marrying a Canaanite woman would raise its own problems, if displacement of the indigenous population is the goal.

As the narrative which will illuminate Lot's character continues, no sooner has the Lord told Abram to pull up roots in Haran and continue on to Canaan and Abram complies with God's order, than a famine sends Abram to Egypt, where he pretends that his wife is his sister, and then, Sarai having been returned to him by a Pharaoh unpleased by the deception, Abram leaves Egypt, "he, and his wife, and all that he had, and Lot with him, into the south." Were it suggested that Lot helped out by advising his uncle to try the wife/sister deception on Pharoah, we would reject that suggestion as wholly implausible, for we know Lot too well. He travels with the family group without adding anything to their understanding of themselves, and since that is how the narrative presents him, that is how readers should expect him to respond when faced with a genuine decision, a real challenge. Lot is not Joseph, tempered in adversity until his soul has become iron, nor Daniel, who, put to the test, would prevail because he has it in him to do so. He is not a bad man, but quick intelligence, steady pursuit of clear goals, courage, and the like are not qualities which the narrative attributes to him.

In Chapter 13 we come to the first decision that Lot has ever been asked to make. It is occasioned by a problem that he and Abram share and that the two of them will have to solve, i.e., "the land was not able to bear" the flocks and herds of both. Abram of course takes the initiative by stating the problem and laying out the options for solving it. Their two establishments will have to separate, but the choice of who goes where he ostentatiously gives to Lot: "if thou wilt take the left hand, then I will go to the right; or if thou depart to the right hand, then I will go to the left." This is not a trick question but a choice offered to Lot. The decision is his call, and he decides.

> Lot lifted up his eyes, and beheld all the plain of Jordan, that it was well watered every where,
> . . . even as the garden of the Lord, like the land of Egypt, as thou comest unto Zoar. 13:10

This is not the acquisitive response of a man bent upon making himself richer than he already is. Rather, it is an aesthetic response, a reaction of spontaneous wonder at the beauty of the place, and it overwhelms his heart because it is God's own beauty, or the image thereof.

When Newman selects as epigraph for this sermon the passage in which Lot "beheld all the plain of Jordan," he interprets the text as indicating Lot's desire for wealth, calling his herds of livestock "a pledge of God's favour," which he forgot when he lusted after the fertile territory he lived in. Lot looked toward Sodom, which "was to go the way of the world" and make riches "the end of life." Yet even as he writes this Newman sees that he is overreaching, because after insisting that "if all this does not in its fulness apply to Lot," which it certainly does not, "his history at least reminds us of what takes place daily in instances which resemble it externally." He then moves to the attack on English corruption of religion which had been his target from the outset. "Do we not support religion for the sake of peace and good order, [and] support it only so far as it secures them?"

The next two sermons in the volume's opening cluster, "Wilfulness of Israel in Rejecting Samuel" and "Saul," are companion pieces that were first preached one week apart in mid-May, 1830. Their substantive connection is this, that the people demanded of Samuel a king to rule over them, and Saul was precisely the sort of king they deserved to have. Newman begins with the postulate that "entire sur-render" to their creator was "an especial duty" demanded of the chosen people, along with the companion observation that the most salient characteristic of Israelite history is "deliberate and obstinate transgression" of that duty. The pun-ishments that they suffered were inflicted not for lazy disobedience or weakness in temptation, but for a "deliberate, shameless presumption" which sent them "run-ning forward just in that very direction in which the providence of God did *not* lead them." The Lord having raised up the prophet Samuel to govern them and hav-ing rescued them from their enemies the Philistines, the Israelites showed their lack of gratitude by demanding "a king like the nations." Their excuse for so doing was the palpable unworthiness of Samuel's sons, which led them to anticipate the problems that would arise if they succeeded their father, and to scotch that nascent problem by crafting a solution of their own devising——an expression of tacit dis-trust of divine governance.

Because they wished to manage their affairs themselves "instead of waiting God's time," God "gave them a king in His anger," an action which in time led to "the dispersion or rather annihilation of the greater part of the tribes." Applying this archetype drawn from salvation history to the England of his own day, Newman sees his Church falling prey to the identical error made by the Israelites, pointing out that "friends of the Church are far more disposed to look out for secular and unauthorized ways of defending her, than to proceed quietly in their ordinary duties, and to trust God to save her." While that may sound like advocacy of inef-fectual quietism, such apparent inaction has always been essential to ensuring "the great deliverances of the Church," and, as Newman says, "the course of Providence is not materially different now." The advice he offers "the true Israel among us" is to trust in God rather than "form plans of our own," because doing so never produces the good effects anticipated from it, and frequently does harm.

The companion sermon, "Saul," explores the character of the king whom Samuel selected to govern the Israelites, "a king *after their own heart*." In wishing for a king of their own, they had a double motive. They were both bored with their tribal situation and jealous of the surrounding tribes, for they were "dazzled with the pomp and splendour of the heathen monarchs." Moreover, there is "a sameness, an absence of hue and brilliancy" in genuine religion, a "plainness," an "austerity" or "sadness," for those who do not love it. This was not the first time the Israelites demanded more excitement, more variety, more spice, since they had soon tired of the heavenly manna in the desert and hankered for the flavorful vegetables, the tangy fruits of Egypt. For similar reasons in Samuel's day they desired a king to sup-ply the perceived deficit. Saul filled the bill well, having the strengths and weak-nesses which "became an eastern monarch," that is, the characteristics which would "secure the fear and submission of his subjects."

Turning from the unmet desires of his wilfully servile subjects to the king himself and his relationship with the Lord through Samuel's mediation, Newman puts the question, why was the Israelites' new king "marked for vengeance" and rejection almost from the start, as Samuel repeatedly warns him? "It would appear," he suggests, "that Saul was never under the abiding influence of religion," however he might be moved at this time or that, as when he goes out dancing with the prophets. Comparing Saul with other individuals in the Old Testament, Newman isolates what seems to him the reason why it is that, "while David is called a man after God's own heart," Saul is firmly "put aside as worthless."

> Some men are inconsistent in their conduct, as Samson; or as Eli, in a different way; and yet may have lived by faith. Others have sudden falls, as David had. Others are corrupted by prosperity, as Solomon. But as to Saul, there is no proof that he had any deep-seated religious principle at all, . . . [for] when we look for evidence of his faith, that is, a practical sense of things unseen, we discover instead a deadness to all considerations not connected with the present world. 3.35–6

If that be the case, which is how it appears to Newman, one is not surprised when Saul "forced himself" to offer the sacrifice intended to ensure the success of his military operation. Offering the sacrifice, which only the Lord's priest was permitted to do, was an illuminating act because it "implied that he was careless about forms, which in this world will ever be essential to things supernatural." In summation, "unbelief and wilfulness," the traits exhibited by the Israelites, are also "the wretched characteristics of Saul's history." Newman concludes the sermon by giving his auditors the opportunity to discover within themselves the acts and attitudes exhibited by Saul: "Surely there is not any one soul here present but what may trace in itself, the elements of sins like his," sins that are specified for their reflective consideration. This is the georgic knot which needs to be tied, lest the sermon be no more than an informational essay.

Passing over "Early Years of David," which is included in the opening set as a positive contrast to the pattern of betrayal that threads itself inexorably through the history of Israel, we come to the final leg of their wrongheaded journey in "Jeroboam." Here, we see the collusion between the people and their king which was featured in "Wilfulness of Israel" and "Saul" becoming a wedding bond, their common will being the intention to ignore and turn away from the direction that divine providence would have them take. After the death of Solomon, his son Rehoboam rejects the Israelites' plea to temper his father's harshness against them, which prompts the ten tribes to break away and form their own kingdom to the north. As Newman states it, after having "obstinately courted and struggled after" the despot they desired, they "found themselves discontented" at being abused by Rehoboam and, rather than suffer their punishment by submission to God's will, they took Jeroboam as king and made him "the leader of their rebellion."

Jeroboam had been a talented and industrious official during Solomon's reign, but when the Lord's prophet Ahijah announced that he would become king over the ten tribes, he took the prophecy as a justification for independent action and attempted to assassinate Solomon, his failure making it prudent to seek protection in Egypt. In what respect were Jeroboam and Israel bound together with one will as husband and wife? Jeroboam attempted to seize the kingship without waiting God's time and means, while the Israelites did not have the patience to endure Rehoboam's refusal of leniency, and this commonality of thought and action is the reason Newman calls Jeroboam "a special emblem of the whole people in the rebellion itself." After that beginning, this king "sinned further and more grievously," because

> When a man begins to do wrong, he cannot answer for himself how far he may be carried on . . . One false step forces him to another, for retreat is impossible. This, which occurs every day, is instanced, first, in the history of the whole people, and then, in the history of Jeroboam. 3.67

What eventually dawned on him as a problem needing solution was this, that the Jewish nation was "not only a kingdom, but a church, a religion as well as a political body," like Newman's England. And Jeroboam found "that in setting up a new kingdom in Israel, he must set up a new religion too," since the Mosaic Law required that men worship in Jerusalem three times a year, and if they revisited Judah to fulfill this obligation, they would soon "return to their former allegiance." The upshot was that "a second false step was necessary to complete the first." Jeroboam therefore set up figures of gold, reminiscent of the golden calf, to mark the boundaries of his kingdom, and established within them new locations for worship. The most telling passage in the sermon as it bears upon the religious situation in England posits the same principle at work in the schismatic innovations of both ages. "Jeroboam's sins," says Newman,

> were not single, or inconsistent with each other, but depended on this principle—that there is no need to attend to the positive laws and the outward forms and ceremonies of religion, so that we attend to the substance . . . He thought he was only altering the discipline of the Church, as we should now call it. 3.69–70

Having dismissed the Levites from their priesthood and appointed other priests not of the tribe of Levi, but from the lowest social ranks, Jeroboam "made it impossible for pious Israelites to remain in the country. The irreligious alone held with him." Thus, the pattern of defection and abandonment, having been once begun, continues to progress from bad to worse. Applying the Israelites' history to his own day, Newman concludes with this conditional, that "if the deeds of Israel and Jeroboam may be taken as types of what has been acted under the Gospel for centuries past, can we doubt that schism, innovation in doctrine, a counterfeit priesthood, sacrilege, and violence, are sins so heinous and crying, that there is no judgment too great for them?"

While the first group of sermons presents the volume's negative example, i.e., betrayal of allegiance to God, the second set makes the turn to the positive emphasis which predominates thereafter. The four sermons of the second cluster were originally written and preached during the three-month span from March to May of 1835. The earliest of these in time of composition, which apparently prompted Newman to continue exploring in the other three the theme which it introduces, is in Volume 3 repositioned to the end of the sequence to provide the strongest conclusion. All four of the sermons share the theme of reciprocal affection between Christ and the fervent Christian, whose religious feelings arise not in self-contemplation, but in meditation on those Gospel texts which show Jesus interacting with his contemporaries. Because these sermons not only share their theme but elaborate it with little variation in viewpoint and emphasis, they can strike a reader as being repetitive. The reason why Newman does not flinch from that danger is that he is attempting to bring truisms, too often repeated from memory instead of being brought to life by meditative attention, back towards the freshness of new-minted truth. Or rather, he is hoping to assist his readers do that for themselves, by providing them how-to-proceed advice.

The first member of the set, "A Particular Providence as Revealed in the Gospel," opens with Newman's observation that while the Old Testament contains "occasional notices" of God's concern for individuals, it is "deficient" in this regard compared to the Gospels. The Old Testament norm is illustrated by Abraham and Moses, since they are addressed as leaders and representatives of the whole people rather than spoken to personally by God, as if for their own sake. To the contrary, it is un-typical for the angel of the Lord to seek out Abraham's Egyptian wife Hagar as she pines in anxious distress by the well in the wilderness, the angel's intent being to give her good counsel in a private domestic dispute (Gen. 16:7–13). Abraham's wife Sarah having asked him to take Hagar to wife because she herself has failed to conceive, the handmaid becomes pregnant and begins lording it over Sarah, who, jealous and angry, "dealt hardly" with Hagar until she fled the household, which did not improve her situation. One could argue that Hagar's pregnancy is important to God because His will is that her son Ishmael shall become "a great nation," but notwithstanding that circumstance, Hagar recognizes that God has singled her out personally for special attention. Her startled, happy cry "Thou God seest me," which Newman adopts as the epigraph of the sermon, points to the New Testament's manifold increase in the particularity of the Lord's solicitous attention.

Latent behind Newman's opening observation one finds this unstated question, why does the New Testament depart from the Old in providing so much evidence of God's active concern for everybody, without regard to whether they are high or low, rich or poor, good or bad? The short answer is that God has since become man. That is the divine act which has made all the difference, nor would it have been possible without human cooperation. Gabriel's question to Mary, whether she is willing to become the mother of the Saviour, is the watershed. Mary's "yes" signifies that she will not stand in the way of God's will. If on the other hand Judas decides to betray Jesus, Jesus can do nothing to stop him. The decision of the individual person has become paramount in God's providential governance, because He has made Himself the hostage of His own creatures. This is an astonishing situation, a wholly new thing.

The difficulty in human perception that the Gospel's revelation attempts to ameliorate is that, although God is invisible, people need to *see* if they are to believe with confident assurance. Newman says that from God's "being invisible," our imaginations have difficulty "attributing" to Him that "tenderness" and "considerateness" which truly are His, "even when our reason is convinced, and we wish to believe accordingly." The solution which the Incarnation has provided for such a difficulty is that, in Jesus, God "has taken upon Him the thoughts and feelings of our own nature, which we all understand *is* capable of personal attachments." Moreover, while fellow feeling goes a long way to establish bonds of love, the lover's sacrifice on behalf of the beloved person, putting himself in danger or suffering distress and loss as evidence of the strong wish to be united, goes the greater distance to elicit answering affection. In this regard, Newman expresses the Lord's generosity in direct address to each particular reader, saying "Thou wast one of those for whom Christ offered up His last prayer, and sealed it with his precious blood," a thought so amazing that "scarce can we refrain from acting Sarah's part," who was prompted to laugh from amazement and perplexity. The Christian is enabled to make tangible for himself such truths as these by joining Christ in prayer "upon the holy mount," prayer that is still the Christian's "inward strength" when he descends to daily duties, "though he is not allowed to tell the vision to those around him."

The second sermon, "Tears of Christ at the Grave of Lazarus," opens with the question, why did Jesus weep for his deceased friend when He already knew that the dead man was soon to leave the tomb, trailing graveclothes from his reanimated body? The question is a good one because it lends itself to meditation not on the miracle-worker Jesus but on the man like you and me, himself moved to weeping by seeing the mourners overcome with grief. Because Jesus is neither the one nor the other but both at once, the Son of God and the son of Mary, it can be difficult for Christians to understand his words and thoughts. To comprehend them we must, says Newman, "feed upon them, and live in them, as if by little and little growing into their meaning." The important thing is to "leave off vague statements about His love" and examine "His particular and actual works," since without doing so we will miss the Gospels' central benefit. Restating the question in another way, why does the Lord of Life need to suffer the rending pain of sorrow when He can, and will, restore Lazarus? Newman's answer is that Jesus assumed a human soul and body "in order that thoughts, feelings, affections, might be His, which could respond to ours and certify to us His tender mercy." When He weeps at Lazarus' grave "from sympathy with Mary's tears," it is nothing less than "the love of God . . . condescending to show it as we are capable of receiving it, in the form of human nature."

Jesus's conduct at Lazarus' tomb is reminiscent of yet different from that of Joseph in Egypt meeting the brothers who had earlier sold him into slavery. As Newman develops the parallel between them, Joseph wished and intended to help his relatives, yet he would do so at no immediate cost to himself because his position gave him invulnerability. But "Christ was bringing life to the dead by His own death," for the fame of raising Lazarus was "the immediate cause of His seizure and crucifixion." What Jesus "has done for all believers, revealing His atoning death yet not explaining it," says Newman, He did for Martha and Mary, walking then silently to the tomb to raise Lazarus, "while they complained that he had been allowed to die." The text which the preacher is commenting on has been dulled by too-frequent hearing without meditative reflection to reanimate it, a deadening which Newman is trying to reverse.

> Contemplating then the fulness of His purpose while now going about a single act of mercy, He said to Martha, "I am the Resurrection and the Life; he that believeth in Me, though he were dead, yet shall he live, and whosoever liveth and believeth in Me, shall never die." 3.137–8

"Bodily Suffering" tries to answer the question, what is the use, the purpose, the reason for physical pain? The Old Testament understands bodily sickness as punishment for sin, as is evident from John's account of the man born blind whom Jesus cured ("Rabbi, who sinned, this man or his parents?" (9:1–3)) and can be inferred from Mark's account of the paralytic man whom Jesus cured ("which of these is easier, your sins are forgiven or pick up your bed and walk?" (2:5–12)). With the New Testament, that explanation is exploded and a wholly different way of understanding bodily suffering takes hold. Scripture had prophecied that the Savior would be "clothed with vesture dipped in blood," the event proved that "the sufferings of the Eternal Word in our nature" was the Atonement for sin, and therefore it cannot be a surprise—Jesus having foretold it clearly and repeatedly—that His followers must take up their cross, that the grain of wheat must fall to the ground and die.

As Newman points out, however, the natural effect of physical pain upon the mind is "to fix our thoughts on ourselves" and make us selfish, in a number of different ways which the sermon specifies. It follows that bodily suffering sets the difficulty to be overcome, the challenge the Christian must meet in order to imitate Jesus. It is a matter of answering affection, persistence in allegiance to the Lord. If properly used, pain "carries on the Christian mind from the thought of self to the contemplation of Christ," and indeed to "that united company of sufferers who follow Him and 'are what He is in this world.'" The necessary mental work is this, to make the presence, the persistence and indeed the wrenching anguish of exquisite suffering "our own voluntary act, by the cheerful and ready concurrence of our own will with the will of God." Says Newman, pain and tribulation are "the most congruous attendants upon those who are called to inherit the benefit of them," where by the phrase most congruous he means "most natural and befitting, harmonizing most fully, with the main Object in the group of sacred wonders on which the Church is called to gaze." The example which Christ gave is clear, so too is that of the Apostles, and beyond that it is up to the individual Christian to summon the faith and endurance in pain that allegiance to Christ requires.

The first three sermons of the group position Jesus firmly in the context that the Gospels narrate, emphasizing the family ties, the commonality of nature between the Son of God and His creatures. Having made those ties palpable through mutual sacrifice and endurance of suffering, Newman concludes the sermon group with "The Humiliation of the Eternal Son," a strictly theological exposition which sets out to explain the necessity, or the intelligibility, the function of the union of the two natures within Jesus, such that He is at once God, incapable of suffering, as well as man, and therefore able to take on the mantle of suffering servant, becoming obedient through his human nature. Here, the persistence of His divine allegiance is most completely operative, for as God, Christ wills our salvation through the Atonement, while, as man, Jesus performs what, as God, He himself wills. Exploring the Gospel passage "Though He were a Son, yet learned He obedience by the things which He suffered," Newman points out that

> Obedience belongs to a servant, but accordance, concurrence, co-operation, are the characteristics of a Son. In His eternal union with God there was no distinction of will and work between Him and His Father . . . But in the days of His flesh, when He had humbled Himself "to the form of a servant," taking on Himself a separate work, and the toil and sufferings incident to a creature, then what had been mere concurrence became obedience . . . He took on Him a lower nature, and wrought in it towards a Will higher and more perfect than it. 3.163

Newman's England, as he describes it, is a catch-as-catch-can religious environment in which individuals gather up "fragments of religious knowledge" by hearing "one thing said in Church," by finding something else "in the Prayer-book," by then picking up another fragment "among religious people," and thereby getting "possession of sacred words" without understanding them. In his incomprehension, a man cobbles together "the various and inconsistent opinions" he has collected and "puts his own meaning upon them," yet his meaning is the flawed notion of "an untaught, not to say a carnal and irreverent mind." As a result, an expression like "the Son of God" can for such a person mean virtually anything, but the odds that it signifies what the Apostles taught are miniscule. One can hardly blame the particular badly-taught Christian, for while "continual meditation" on the Gospel texts would help, he will also require "diligent use of the Church's instruction." This is the sore point for Newman, because the Church's instruction is often less, and less reliable, than it ought to be. In the theological lamentation which closes the sermon, Newman wonders

> How long will that complicated Error last under which our Church now labours? How long are human traditions of modern date to obscure, in so many ways, the majestic interpretation of Holy Writ which the Church Catholic has inherited from the age of the Apostles? . . . Surely in vain have we escaped from the superstitions of the middle ages, if the corruptions of a rash and self-trusting philosophy spread over our faith! 3.171–2

The third cluster contains only two sermons, but these are important since they investigate two related opposites, the distressing imperfections of professed Christians, and the confidence that the glory Christ has revealed continues its invisible work of transforming hearts and minds. The first of these, "The Visible Church an Encouragement to Faith," is interesting chiefly for its limited success in finding such encouragement specifically within the visible church. Newman repeatedly informs us that the *invisible* church gives comfort, but that is not what the sermon sets out to do. The problem he grapples with is that we cannot see the reality which is being looked for. "God alone sees the heart," says Newman, and faithful Christians, although some kindred spirits "are revealed to them in a measure," some "one or two" being "given them to rejoice in," there are "not many even of these." It is the loneliness of the journey which raises the desire for greater encouragement.

Difficult to follow because of the mismatch between its ostensible goal and the nature of the evidence brought in support, "The Visible Church . . ." (Sept 14, 1834) is made easier to understand by the two sermons which precede it in Volume 3, both of them written in the year after the sermon they clarify, both of them addressing issues common to all three. The first of these, "Contest Between Truth and Falsehood in the Church" (17 May, 1835), points out that the warfare between Christ's flock and the world was very quickly "transferred into the Church itself," although even in Newman's century, when it can be "plainly seen, men will not see it," since they refuse to admit that Christ's Kingdom "is like a net that gathers of every kind," good and bad alike. They therefore have "invented an Invisible Church . . . peopled by saints only." Newman identifies a serious oversight here, one followed by an equally serious error which wrongly attempts to right the situation which the oversight itself creates. Five months after composing "Contest Between Truth and Falsehood . . . ," Newman writes "The Church Visible and Invisible" (25 Oct, 1835), which pursues further the mistake which the earlier sermon had briefly reflected on, and this adjacent sermon is crucially helpful for contexting "The Visible Church. . . ." Here, Newman repeats the observation that, from the Apostles' time until the present, the Church has been "the seat of unbelief and unholiness as well as of true religion." Now the important thing that Newman does in this sermon is to provide the definitional clarity which is essential if we are to be accurate in evaluating "The Visible Church an Encouragement to Faith."

There is no problem distinguishing between the Visible and the Invisible Church, says Newman, so long as we know what we mean by the distinction. The body of the elect "as it already exists in Paradise" can properly be called the Invisible Church because "this blessed consummation takes place in the unseen world." To speak in this way does not "make two Churches." Rather, "we only view the Christian body as existing in the world of spirits; and the present Church Visible so far as it really has part and lot in the same blessedness." Some pages further on, Newman, arguing against those who invent an Invisible Church in order to keep out of it the sinners who would infect and corrupt it, points out that the Church "cannot be in a worse condition" now than it was in during Christ's time, "yet He expressly assures us" that, however faulty or wicked the Scribes and Pharisees, they were to be obeyed in what they taught. "Surely, then," he continues, "we may infer, that, however fallen the Church now is from what it once was . . . it still has the gift . . . to convey and withdraw the Christian privileges."

When we come to "The Visible Church an Encouragement to Faith" in Volume 3, it thus has been established that the net-that-gathers-of-every-kind Church is doing Christ's work, which is saving sinners. There remains the question, because the presence, and perhaps even the preponderance of sinners in the Visible Church is dispiriting to Christians struggling to live the devout life, what encouragement can they expect to find, precisely in the imperfect Church they find discouraging? From the very start, Newman throws the sermon off balance by giving it a title badly matched with its epigraph, the *Epistle to the Hebrews*' shout of triumph, "Wherefore seeing we are also encompassed about with so great a cloud of witnesses. . . ." While these witnesses give encouragement, it is provided by the Invisible Church, not the Visible one. In like manner, the second paragraph begins "And much is needed . . . as a remedy against unbelief . . . the vision of the Saints of God, and of the Kingdom of Heaven . . . because [His faithful] are few, and faint for company." They do indeed, yet "the vision of the Saints of God" is the communion of the blessed souls who are invisible in Paradise, not the visible church on earth that the title promises would provide encouragement.

Eventually the sermon's long-delayed definition of the Visible Church is pro-vided. It is "that one only company which Christians know as yet," set up at Pentecost with the Apostles for rulers.

> In this Visible Church . . . the Church Invisible is gradually moulded and matured. It is formed slowly and variously by the Blessed Spirit of God, in the instance of this man and that, who belong to the general body. But all of these blessed fulfilments of God's grace are as yet parts of the Visible Church; they grow from it . . . there is no Invisible Church yet formed; it is but a name as yet; a name given to those who are hidden, and known to God only, and as yet but half formed, the unripe and gradually ripening fruit which grows on the stem of the Church Visible. As well might we attempt to foretell the blossoms which will at length turn to account and ripen for the gathering, and then counting up all these and joining them together in our minds, call them by the name of a tree, as attempt now to asso-ciate in one the true elect of God. They are scattered about amid the leaves of that Mystical Vine which is seen, and receive their nurture from its trunk and branches. They live on its Sacraments and its Ministry; they gain light and salvation from its rites and ordinances; they communicate with each other through it. 3.240–1

Yet these Christians can see all around them much "to hurt and offend them" because of the bad example of imperfection within the Church, "and hence it is that religious men need some consolation to support them, which the Visible Church seems . . . not to supply." This frames the crucial point one expects the writer to deliver, and Newman heightens our attention further by asking, "Is the Church which they see really no consolation . . . except as contemplated by faith in respect of its invisible gifts?" He then attempts to answer in the affirmative.

The paragraph which follows this framing assertion is an impressive figurative invention based on the nature of physical light and its effects upon the eye. Satan cannot "quench or darken" the Church's light because "even opaque bodies trans-mit rays." The Holy Spirit guarantees that the Church bears "the visible signs of its hidden privilege."

> Viewed at a little distance, its whole surface will be illuminated, though the light really streams from apertures which might be numbered. The scattered witnesses thus become, . . . [as the epigraph says] "a cloud," like the Milky Way in the heavens. 3.243

The Milky Way is a cosmically telling metaphor, but what follows this figural tri-umph is a strained attempt to find evidence to support the thesis. The argument continually slides off to one side, because the sermon repeatedly finds encourage-ment in something which is not the Visible Church. Sometimes "visible" alters in its meaning from the sense in which Newman had employed it, so that it now refers to the painted saints pictured on the walls or seen in the stained glass windows of the building also called "church." This glancing-off phenomenon evidences a weak argument that does not deliver what the sermon promises.

The two lengthy paragraphs that follow fail to advance the argument. The first revisits the irrelevant theme that "the spirits of the just made perfect encourage him," again offering consolation that the distressed Christian can find by gazing back upon earlier times, or forward to Paradise. But the subsequent paragraph transitions to hopeful news by saying that the despondent faithful are "especially excited by the Church of Christ." This is surprising, for if it be so exciting, why is the evidence deferred so long? Newman asks, "What is that Church but a pledge and proof of God's never-dying love?" It is that, to be sure, yet one begins to suspect that a Christian will need to seek encouragement solely from his faith, rather than from any more palpable supports. Yes, the Church is "a pledge and proof" of God's love, and it is still in operation. But mere continuance in the world cannot alleviate the isolation and loneliness from which the sermon had promised relief.

It is as though Newman has been deferring the evidence he is uncomfortable discussing, but finally he broaches the subject: the bishops, the Church leaders, those under whose guidance the Visible Church operates. Every bishop, Newman says, descends through a spiritual birth from Saints Peter and Paul. And if "at various time the bishops [have] acted unworthily," yet for all their negligence, incompetence, or worse, "they are not the less inspiring an object to the believing mind" since the believer looks beyond the visible world and recognizes "in each of them the earnest of His promise, 'I will never leave thee' . . . Here then, surely, is somewhat of encouragement for us amid our loneliness and weakness." To the contrary, rogue or lazy bishops cannot but contribute to the loneliness and sense of helplessness. As Newman continues, every bishop "is the promise of a bold fight and a good confession and a cheerful martyrdom now, if needful, as was instanced in those of old time." It is difficult to read this passage, written in September, 1834, and not be reminded of Newman's statement near the front of the opening number of *Tracts for the Times* (concerning the "Ministerial Commission"), published just one year earlier, in September of 1833, which asserts that the care of the churches is the bishops' glory, and "not one of us would wish in the least to deprive them" of their toils. And if it should come to that, though it would be a "black event" for the country, with respect to the bishops themselves, "we could not wish them a more blessed termination of their course, than the spoiling of their goods, and martyrdom" (Vol. I, p. 1). Those with any sensitivity to the mother tongue and experience of Newman's skill as a satirist would recognize in phrases like "wish in the least to deprive," and "could not wish them a more blessed termination," leading toward "the spoiling of their goods" as prologue to their literal butchering upon the steps of their episcopal residences a rather jaundiced view of the Anglican bishops, one which must surely limit their ability to offer comfort. On the other hand, there were admirable Anglican bishops in Newman's day, those he calls "our living Apostles." Lesser bishops he calls "descendants" of the Apostles, who "lived to the world" and thought their office "secular and civil," though when they flourished Newman's prose never does say. In any case, his living Apostles have the exemplary power to remind us of "the more favoured of their line," who "at various times" defended the Faith well. In summation, the bishops appear to have given a mixed performance, some good and others less so, and thus the consolation they provide to isolated, lonely Christians will be similarly mixed.

Newman moves towards the sermon's conclusion by saying that the Sacred Services of the Church can be made to offer "a support" for our faith and hope. But this suggestion is vulnerable to the response that the Church's liturgy is not the Visible Church, nor those in it, but the Prayer-book's inanimate testimony to how Christians ought to worship. "I am speaking all along," says Newman, "of the help given us by sensible objects." Yet the liturgy being celebrated by a Christian community is different from "sensible objects." Unfortunately, this sermon's fault line, which runs between the title and the epigraph, leads one to expect precisely that slippage between the meaning of "sensible objects" and of liturgical actions. When Newman tells us that "the very disposition of the building, the subdued light, the aisles, the Altar, with its pious adornments, are figures of things unseen" which stimulate our faith, he is not wrong. But he forgets what he had promised us the sermon would deliver.

While "The Visible Church . . ." addresses a state of feeling, i.e., the spiritual loneliness of individuals, it is followed by a very different sermon, "The Gift of the Spirit," which hopes to clarify the meaning of the "glory" texts in Scripture. There are certain passages in the Old Testament which either describe or allude to the glory of the Lord, but it is the Gospels and Epistles of the New wherein one finds the majority of these texts, which articulate the essence of the mutual cooperation between the triune God and humanity. In them, the word "glory," theologically central to Christ's redemption but difficult to understand, has a conundrum quality which makes it all but impervious to normal understanding. And yet, ignoring or misusing the glory texts because of their obscurity has serious practical results. As Newman says, people ignorant that the gifts of grace are "unseen, supernatural, and mysterious" too easily give Scripture's "high and glowing expressions" that "rash, irreverent, and self-exalting" meaning which those inclined towards "religious ecstacy" cannot resist, while "sober and sensible-minded" persons, unable to understand the texts which others misinterpret, "acquiesce in the notion" that the gift of the Holy Ghost, i.e., the gift of glory, was "peculiar to the Apostles' day," and now only makes us "decent and orderly members of society." Reflecting upon the similarity of these equally unfortunate responses, Newman says

> The mind catches at the words of life, and tries to apprehend them; and being debarred their true meaning, takes up with this or that form of error, as the case may be, in the semblance of truth, by way of compensation. 3.269

"The Gift of the Spirit" attempts to explicate the Bible's glory texts with sufficient clarity to help its readers avoid these twin errors. Such an undertaking cannot easily succeed because, as Newman admits, "the gift is denoted in Scripture by the vague and mysterious term 'glory,' and all the descriptions we can give of it can only, and should only, run out into a mystery."

To produce this reading, I have selected from the many glory texts Newman has introduced a manageable few, through which I hope to clarify the Scriptural meaning of glory. I use *Jerusalem Bible* translations as being more intelligible than the *King James* rendering. For example, where the *King James* renders *Exodus*, 34:5, "And the Lord descended in the cloud, and stood with him there, and proclaimed the name of the Lord," the *Jerusalem Bible* has "And Yahweh descended in the form of a cloud, and Moses stood with him there," which is more easily understood. To begin, no Old Testament text is more important toward an understanding of glory than the *Exodus* account of Moses' face glowing after he talks with Yahweh. Descending from Mt. Sinai with the tablets of the Law, Moses did not know "the skin of his face was radiant," that is, he was unaware that the exchange between a divine and a human mind had produced an unusual visual phenomenon. When Aaron and the sons of Israel saw him from a distance, they were struck with fear and "would not venture near him" until Moses called them, when they, being reassured, "came closer, and he passed on to them all the orders that Yahweh had given him." Only after Moses had finished relaying the Lord's commandments did he "put a veil over his face," the implication being that the visible glory was functional in transferring the Lord's Meaning with the Lord's Authority. Every time Moses "went into Yahweh's presence," he removed the face-veil, thus opening himself to the divine splendor. In *Exodus*, "glory" enables the reception and dissemination of religious truth.

The Gospel text that most resembles the *Exodus* account is Jesus' Transfiguration, which Newman recognizes as "of a doctrinal nature" since it is "a figurative exhibition" of glory, being "a vision of the glorious kingdom" Christ "set up on earth on His coming." About a week after telling the Apostles that "some standing here" would not see death "till they see the Kingdom of God," Jesus took Peter, James and John "into a high mountain apart," where a scene ensued which is a variation on the theme of the *Exodus* narrative. In the *Jerusalem Bible*'s rendering of the Transfiguration (*Luke*, 9: 28–36), Jesus' "face was changed and his clothing became brilliant as lightning," the important difference between this and *Exodus* being that Moses received the glory from Yahweh, whereas in the Transfiguration not only Jesus' face but also his clothing becomes radiant. That is, light radiates from Jesus' face, yet it also radiates through and brightly illumines his garments. Then "suddenly" Moses and Elijah are present "talking to him," not about the Law, but its fulfilment: "his passing which he was to accomplish in Jerusalem."

Here, the Son of God stands in the position of Yahweh, who is the source of the power and glory which are reflected or transmitted to the human messengers Moses and Elijah, "appearing in glory" along with him. Peter, James and John do not hang back in fear, as do Aaron and the sons of Israel. Though they are "heavy with sleep," they prove equal to the challenge, for they remained awake and saw his glory "and the two men." Moses and Elijah are just that, men, simply human beings "standing with" Christ—where the Apostles themselves will very soon be called upon to stand. While Peter expresses wonder and suggests that they raise "three tents" in honor of the resplendent tableau they have witnessed, "a cloud came and covered them with shadow," and from the cloud is heard God's voice, exactly as in Jesus' baptism, saying "This is my Son, the Chosen one. Listen to him." That is, Jesus is both the message ("This is") and the messenger ("Listen to") of the divine power and glory.

My third witness from among the many mentioned briefly by Newman is Saint Paul, both in his conversion and in two of his Epistles. Going his way to Damascus, Saul of Tarsus did not, like Moses, have good relations with the Lord. He was "breathing threats to slaughter the Lord's disciples," when "just before he reached the city," a light from heaven surrounded him and a voice asked "Why are you persecuting me?" In Moses' experience, the heavenly power transferred the divine radiance to his face, but Saul is blinded by it. He is in a worse plight than Aaron and the Israelites, who retained their sight, i.e., their willingness to accept the word of God, while Saul's mental state was just the reverse and required strong medicine to cure. When Ananias put his hands upon Saul, the "scales fell away from [his] eyes and he could see again," his spiritual disfunction having been removed. The "scales" which fell from Saul's eyes reappear in the form of a "veil" in II Corinthians, not now a face- covering but a mind-shrouding artifact that intercepted the radiance of divine truth. Although Newman does not examine the parallel being presented here, Saint Paul's "veil" over the Israelites' minds insulates their understandings, thus preventing them from seeing in Jesus the promised Messiah.

St. Paul contrasts the radiance on the face of Moses, "which they could not bear looking at," with the brightness "which comes from the Holy Spirit." Further, the veil that protected the Israelites from the brightness on Moses' face has never been removed from the faithless Jews, for "Christ alone can remove it," as Christ alone could take the scales from Paul's own eyes. That veil will not be removed until the Jews "turn to the Lord," for Jesus cannot do it without their own cooperation. Here is another negative example of divine allegiance, God's offer of help rejected by His own people. St. Paul contrasts the Jews' blindness to divine light against the Gospel's freedom, for "where the Spirit of the Lord is," impediments are removed. Describing with great clarity the action of glory, Paul continues:

> And we, with our unveiled faces reflecting like mirrors the brightness of the Lord, all grow
> brighter and brighter as we are turned into the image that we reflect; this is the work of the
> Spirit. II *Cor.* 3: 14–18

Here, Paul is describing our transformation, from mirroring Christ to becoming ourselves His image, such that His glory becomes intrinsic to own essence, for that is
the Spirit's "work."

In the subsequent chapter of II *Corinthians*, Paul once again contrasts the
closed minds of unbelievers, who cannot grasp Christ's glory, with the spiritual state
of faithful Christians: "It is the same God that said, 'Let there be light, shining out
of darkness,' who has shone in our minds to radiate the light of the knowledge of
God's glory, the glory on the face of Christ" (II *Cor.*, 4: 3–6). Here one sees that
the Father, the Son and the Spirit are all called into action in Paul's account, for
the theological truth is that they interpenetrate in their operations on our behalf.

Perhaps more than any other New Testament writer, Paul has the ability to
articulate the tangled and elusive sense of "glory," as when he tells the Ephesians,
"May the Father of glory, give you a spirit of wisdom and perception of what is
revealed, to bring you to full knowledge of him." Although glory is not identical
with wisdom, perception and knowledge, it is connected with them through the
substance of "what is revealed." Continuing, Paul tells them "May he enlighten the
eyes of your mind so that you can see what hope his call holds for you," above all
"the rich glories he has promised the saints will inherit," and, accompanying and
intermingled with those rich glories, "how infinitely great is the power that he has
exercised for us believers," evidence of his power being God's use of it to raise Christ
from the dead, which in Newman's characteristic vocabulary is an *earnest* of his
promise to raise us, too, from death. Again in his epistle's third chapter, Paul prays
on behalf of the Ephesians:

> Out of his infinite glory, may he give you the power through his Spirit for your hidden self
> to grow strong, so that Christ may live in your hearts through faith, and then, planted in
> love and built on love, you will with all the saints have strength to grasp the breadth and
> the length, the height and the depth; until, knowing the love of Christ, which is beyond
> all knowledge, you are filled with the utter fullness of God. 3: 16–20

Newman's "Gift of the Spirit" gives a long catalog of glory texts, an accumulation
which runs towards a summary of the various "characteristics or titles" of glory.
These include

> Illumination, the heavenly gift, the Holy Ghost, the Divine Word, the powers of the world
> to come; which all mean the same thing, viewed in different lights. 3.263

The reality they hope to articulate Newman calls "a present entrance into the next
world," transforming Christians into "ministers round the throne of their recon-

ciled Father." That being so, we have an "insight into St. Paul's anxiety" to ensure that Christ's followers understand "the riches" of their inheritance, which "the natural man" is unable to discern.

As if to balance its opening cluster of four sermons which narrate Israel's turning away from allegiance to God, Volume 3 concludes with four sermons exhorting Christians to persist in prayer, that being the key to strengthening the bond of allegiance between themselves and Christ. The first two members of the set, "The Daily Service" and "The Good Part of Mary," first preached one week apart in late 1834, are companion pieces attacking the widespread opinion that while it is appropriate to attend Church on Sundays, any substantial commitment to prayer beyond that is archaic and unnecessary. The epigraph of "The Daily Service," as rendered by the *Jerusalem Bible* in English of our own day, is "Do not stay away from the meetings of the community, as some do, but encourage others to go," wherein the potential laggard is exhorted to pray more strenuously and along with others. The argument of the sermon is framed by Newman's assertion that the early Christians were engaged in "continual prayer" and that St. Paul "binds their example" on us, as well as by his rhetorical opponent's objection to that view: "But it will be said, 'Times are altered; . . . what was a duty then, need not be a duty now, even though St. Paul happens to enjoin it on those whom he addresses.'" That is the point of disagreement between Newman and the views of the age, which he answers, first, by the practical action of initiating observance of the Daily Service in his parish church, and second, by explaining in this sermon his reasons for doing so.

Chief among Newman's reasons for beginning the Daily Service is his feeling "that we were very unlike the early Christians" to go on without it, and that it was his business to give his parishoners "an opportunity of observing it," which would not happen unless he "set the example." Among the objections he hopes to overcome, "It is commonly said, when week-day prayers are spoken of, 'You will not get a congregation, or you will get but a few.'" To this he replies that "they whom Christ has brought near Himself to be the Stewards of His Mysteries depend on no man; rather, after His pattern, they are to draw men after them." As for his brother Ministers, Newman reminds them that "what He is really, such are we in figure; what He is meritoriously, such are we instrumentally," and as for measuring the real effects of their actions by appearances, "If we wait till all the world are worshippers, we must wait till the world is new made." Newman knows that the views he is advocating appear "strained and unnatural" to some, to others "formal, severe, and tending to bondage," but this cannot be helped, for "Christ's commands will seem to be a servitude, and His privileges will be strange, till we act upon the one and embrace the other."

In summation, Newman advises us to take Christ's words "simply" and begin to pray. Those who do so will "at length find persevering prayer, praise, and intercession, neither bondage nor barrenness." The inherent difficulty, stated here not for the first time in *Parochial Sermons*, is that the Gospel's good tidings do not seem good to those without the heart to abandon sin, and since no one by nature has this good heart, nor can obtain it even under grace "except gradually," there will always be "a degree of bondage in the Gospel, till, by obeying the Law and creating within us a love of God and holiness, we, by little and little," by perseverance, "enter into the meaning of His promises."

"The Good Part of Mary" continues the same line of argument as that opened by "The Daily Service," making the case for as much withdrawal from workaday affairs as one's state in life will permit. Newman recognizes that "active business" and "quiet adoration" are equally acceptable to God, that both Martha and Mary "glorify Him in their own line, whether of labour or of quiet," so long as their service is "from love of Him." And yet, as the epigraph reminds us, Christ rebuked Martha by explaining that "one thing is needful" and that Mary's "good part" will not be taken from her in order that she might serve tables and wash dishes. How did the division of labour between them occur? Not entirely from choice, for Martha was the older and therefore head of the household, Mary the younger and so not expected to take charge, and differing temperaments doubtless contributed something too. Surveying the society around him, Newman reflects that those most easily able to undertake Mary's exercise of "quiet adoration" are the old, children who have as yet to assume secular responsibility, the unmarried, who have more freedom to choose how to spend their time, the Priests of God, and along with these, "the spirits of the just made perfect," who from heaven join in prayer with them.

In the historical record, during its earlier centuries "Mary's portion was withheld from the Church" because of the violent persecutions which it endured in that era. But since that early time, "vast multitudes" of Christians have devoted themselves to adoration. What of Newman's English contemporaries? His view is that "if there be an age when Mary's portion" is not only ignored, but "decried," that age is "so far a stranger to the spirit of the Gospel." Long ago, even in Martha, holy woman though she was,

> we seem to witness, as in type, the rash unchristian way in which this age disparages devotional services. Do we never hear it said, that the daily Service of the Church is unnecessary? Is it never hinted that it is scarcely worth while to keep it up unless we get numbers to attend it? . . . Is it never objected, that a partially-filled Church is a discouraging sight, as if, after all, our Lord Jesus had chosen the many and not the few to be His true disciples?
> 3.332–3

Surely something is wrong when the defenders of Anglicanism "recommend the Church on the mere plea of its activity, its popularity, and its visible usefulness," which is a kind of Spirit of Martha run amok. Moreover, such busy pursuit of practical results is doomed to failure, since, says Newman, "It is mere infatuation if we think to resist the enemies who are at our doors, if our Churches remain shut, and we give up to prayer but a few minutes of the day."

While the first two members of the sermon group argue against a systemic disregard for communal or contemplative prayer, the second pair, "Religious Worship a Remedy for Excitements" and "Intercession," tacitly narrow the reading audience from the general community to individuals who will find the advice they offer helpful. "Religious Worship a Remedy . . ." opens with the analogy between bodily pain, which "throws the mind off its balance," and indisposition of the soul, an affliction which "takes us off from the clear contemplation of the next world, ruffles us, and makes us restless." Whether they be secular or religious, the "proper antidote" for these spiritual indispositions is divine worship. One great benefit of "stated worship," says Newman, is that it interferes with "the urgency" of worldly excitements. For instance, the public Service "is of a certain length, and cannot be interrupted; and it is long enough to calm and steady the mind." This is a benefit of inestimable value to people who would otherwise be "drawn into the great whirlpool of time and sense."

Shifting from secular to religious excitements, Newman contrasts the habitual calm of a Christian who has always been at work to improve his "Gospel privileges" against the "agitating surprise," the "vehemence of joy" felt by a recent convert to the faith. That is why "one can never be sure of a new convert," for in that unusual state of mind his emotions "have more sway" than reason or conscience, and his feelings "may hurry him away, just as a wind might do in a wrong direction." Dramatizing that unstable state in an apt metaphor, Newman says "He is balanced on a single point, on the summit of an excited mind, and he may easily fall." The sermonist next wonders how the early Christians managed to keep themselves stable when they certainly felt that kind of vehemence, and how over a millenium and a half the Church "was preserved from those peculiar affections of mind and irregularities of feeling and conduct which now torment us like an ague." Part of the answer is that God's providence "controlling the heart" saved the early Church from enthusiasm, while another factor was the persecutions of the time. But the "more ordinary means" which provided them stability, one that is still available today, was "the course of religious Services," which calm, soothe, direct and purify "the restless and excited mind." On the other hand, the mind of schism and dissent is different, because it is inherently unstable, being "full of self-importance, irreverence, display, tumult" and like expressions of false religion. There is no cure for those individuals who love their affliction. In summation, Newman counsels us that if anyone is "desirous of gaining comfort to his soul, of bringing Christ's presence to his heart," and helping to bring about wonderful things for the whole world, "Let him pray; especially let him intercede," which is the segue into the last sermon of the group.

"Intercession" begins with an epigraph which reads, in pertinent part, "watching thereunto with all perseverance and supplication for all saints" (*Hebrews*, 6:18), which in modern translation is "Never get tired of staying awake to pray for all the saints." Newman calls intercession the characteristic of Christian worship because "if Christians are to live together, they will pray together; and united prayer is necessarily of an intercessory character," since it is offered for each other, and for oneself as belonging to the whole. Intercession is the special duty of the sincere Christian, for he alone is in a condition to offer it: "Saul the persecutor obviously could not intercede like St. Paul the Apostle." Christ died to make intercessory prayer possible, says Newman, for he died to "bestow upon" His faithful "that privilege which implies or involves all the others, and brings him into nearest resemblance to Himself, the privilege of Intercession." Whoever fails to exercise it "has not risen to the conception of his real place among created beings."

Praying for pardon is necessary, of course, but the observant Christian has "a capacity for higher things," having been "taken into the confidence and counsels of his Lord and Saviour." Yet it is best that those who "are so gifted" do not know for certain that they are. They should instead think of the gift as "lodged in the Church of which they are but members," without being concerned about their particular share in it. But while this helps to safeguard humility, it should not lighten the sense of responsibility for others, since prayer can affect their eternal destiny.

> How can we answer to ourselves for the souls who have, in our time, lived and died in sin; the souls that have been lost and are now waiting for judgment, the infidel, the blasphemer, the profligate, the covetous, the extortioner; or those again who have died with but doubtful signs of faith, the death-bed penitent, the worldly, the double-minded, the ambitious, the unruly, the trifling, the self-willed, seeing that, for what we know, we were ordained to influence or reverse their present destiny and have not done it? 3.336

Helping to clean up such spiritual Augean stables as these through intercessory prayer, Newman implies, is not flight from but practical effort within the temporal world wherein Christians are called to use their talents for the good of the community.

CHAPTER 4

Newman's
Sermonic Rhetoric

Aristotle calls rhetoric the "the faculty of observing in any given case the available means of persuasion." He distinguishes between its two modes, i.e., things which "are there at the outset," such as witnesses, evidence and written contracts, and those which are "supplied by the speaker." Contrasting these two modes, Aristotle says that "the one kind has merely to be used, the other has to be invented" (*Rhetoric* 1355b, Trans. Roberts). Lucretius relies upon the testimony of Epicurus as the single witness to the truth of *De rerum natura*, although Lucretius himself must invent the persuasive argument by selecting and arranging the pertinent evidence taken from his witness. Wordsworth on the other hand relies upon invention pure and simple, drawing upon his own experience for the argument of *The Prelude*. *Parochial Sermons'* rhetoric closely resembles Lucretius' approach, for its persuasive power derives from Scripture, the epigraph standing as textual witness to the divine truth each sermon presents. However, Newman himself must craft the interrogation proper, the specific manner of making-evident the epigraph's spiritual insight.

Thirteen years after publication of *Parochial Sermons*, Newman described his sermonic rhetoric in a lecture which advocates it as a pattern for Christian preachers to follow ("University Preaching"). It is a model consisting of two pieces of procedural advice, followed by a summary of the sermon generating process that works best. First, a sermon needs a single focus: "As a marksman aims at the target and its bull's-eye, and at nothing else, so the preacher must have a definite point before him, which he has to hit." Those who have "one object definitely before them" find it easier to direct all their efforts towards it. "Diction, elocution" and "rhetorical power" should not be sought out, because "display dissipates" the energy which should rather be "concentrated and condensed" (189–90).

Second, Newman advises the preacher to be earnest, for "earnestness creates earnestness in others by sympathy" and provides "a powerful natural instrument" to amplify the force of divine truth. As Aristotle says, the speaker's character "may almost be called the most effective means of persuasion he possesses" (1356a), and Newman concurs, for "the common sense of the world decides that it is safer . . . to commit oneself to the judgment of men of character, than to any considerations addressed merely to the feelings or the reason." Yet the preacher should aim not at being earnest, but "at his *object*, which is to do some spiritual good to his hearers," and that will "*make* him earnest" (190–2). He condenses these two pieces of good advice into a single emphatic analogy of the preacher's task:

> It is said, that, when a man has to cross an abyss by a narrow plank thrown over it, it is his wisdom, not to look at the plank, along which lies his path, but to fix his eyes steadily on the point in the opposite precipice, at which the plank ends. It is by gazing at the object which he must reach, and ruling himself by it, that he secures to himself the power of walking to it straight and steady. 192–3

Similarly, no one becomes earnest by aiming at being so, but by "meditating on the motives, and by drinking at the sources, of earnestness" (193).

Newman concludes his advice by giving an overview of a sermon generating process that an aspiring preacher should follow. First, select as the sermon's focus some distinct fact, scene, truth, doctrine or principle. If it is "some portion of the divine message" it will be sufficient for the purpose, because however "elementary" or "trite" it may be, it will have "a dignity such as to possess him, and a virtue to kindle him, and an influence to subdue and convert those to whom it goes forth from him." The second step is to study the subject thoroughly, dwelling upon it in order to acquire "an habitual understanding of it" which will help him compose. Third, the sermonist should "employ himself, as the one business of his discourse, to bring home to others, and to leave deep within them, what he has, before he began to speak to them, brought home to himself" (198–9).

Newman's rhetoric is a blend of Aristotle's two modes of argument, for if on the one hand he deploys Scriptural testimony "there at the outset" in the form of epigraphs, on the other hand he invents arguments by interrogating and thus enriching the epigraphs' testimony. He gives weight and force to texts whose very familiarity tends to rob them of impact, such that the sermonist's challenge is to elicit a fresh understanding of them. This stage of his practice is unclear until it be examined, for although the advice to "leave deep within" a sermon's audience the insights the preacher has already "brought home" to himself is lucid in principle, illustrative examples can help to show us how Newman does that. Such is the intention of this chapter. Volume 4 consists of four groups of thematically connected sermons, from which four pairs, one pair from each of the volume's sermon groups, will act as demonstration samples.

The first pair is taken from the first sermon cluster, the leitmotif of which is evident in the opening sermon's title "The Strictness of the Law of Christ." This part of the volume attacks self-satisfaction, the presumption that the thoughts and actions which please us should please our Creator. "Acceptance of Religious Privileges Compulsory," challenges an instinctive human demand, the freedom to make our own decisions. Compulsion being offensive, the parable of the Great Supper in St. Luke's Gospel, which provides an epigraph, "Go out into the highways and hedges and compel them to come in," is an affront to human expectation. This insult is more starkly insisted upon in Matthew's version, wherein the guest who lacks a wedding garment is not simply dismissed, but harshly condemned. Heightening for readers the violation of our expectation of fairness, Newman says we might suppose the guest would answer his host's question how he came there, "'I was forced in;' but our Saviour says 'And he was speechless,' and pronounces his everlasting punishment." The implication is that we are compelled to accept the religious privileges imposed upon us without our consent, "for the use of which we are answerable, for the misuse of which we shall be condemned." The same "awful and startling" doctrine can be found in the parable of the talents, wherein the one who buried his gift "seems to have had some such thoughts about fairness and justice, as the natural man so often indulges in now,—-some idea of being quits and even with [his master], if he left his gift alone," because his lord was "hard to please, having his own views of right and duty, and unreasonable." Who is it that proclaims this law of our nature, "the duty of being accountable," but the gentle Jesus, the mild and beneficent Saviour, who says about Judas, "it had been better for that man if he had not been born." Yet Judas "was born, he was suffered to betray, and he was condemned," however unfairly he may have thought himself treated.

Having used the epigraph to generate his invention of the sermon's opening, Newman tells his readers how he means to proceed: "Now, I shall enlarge somewhat upon the general state of the case," and show how Christians are "especially interested" in it. To do that, he examines the parallel between our birth into the world and the Christian's "new birth" in baptism. They are similar because either birth makes us "an unwilling recipient of a gift." Our birth in the world is "to the pride of reflecting but irreligious minds" unacceptable. If they refuse to submit, they have not many options. For the sake of reader relations they have only two, since the sermonist would lose his audience if, at the outset of a complex comparison, he suggested six or seven possibilities. Their first option is suicide, or "rushing out of life by self-inflicted violence, from the frantic hope that perchance they have power over their own being." The folly of this becomes evident when they find themselves "sentient, conscious, independent beings" still, but without the bodies which afforded them the capacity to act for themselves. Now, they have "no power over the principle of their life, which rests upon the will of Him alone, who called them into being." Their other option is to drift down the stream of life aimlessly, never realizing that their circumstances "are but conditions appointed by Almighty God," talents and opportunities they are bound "to take, use, and improve."

In terms of reader propinquity, the direction of this sermon is from the remote to the near, i.e., from figures in parables and hypothetical persons who waste their lives, to the reader's intimate situational concerns. Making that transition, Newman explores the other half of the parallel he is investigating: "Such is our condition as men; it is the same as Christians. . . . We as little choose our religion as we choose to be born." Infants are never asked whether they want to be baptized, but receive the Sacrament nonetheless. Newman imagines a Christian lamenting having been baptized because it puts him at greater risk should he fall into sin. The reality is that we have been baptized and can refuse neither the privilege nor the responsibility of it. Rather than shrink back from the burden, we should instead "comfort ourselves with the privilege . . . the fulness of the aid given us to help us," and do our best to live worthily. As with baptism, so with education, Newman tells an audience born into Anglican families. "We cannot stand aloof, and say we will keep our judgment unbiassed, and decide for ourselves." Instead, we have to employ our talents and prove their worth "by deeds, not by arguments."

Newman's comments on Christian baptism and education having comprised the second of the sermon's four sections, the third, more remote from his readers, provides evidence that compulsion by the Church is "still more urgent and extensive." He gives "a few instances" from Church history to impress upon his audience "the principle on which" such compulsion is founded. First, the Apostles baptized entire households at a stroke—grown persons, slaves, children, everyone. Second, the early Church brought to priestly ordination such as had "the necessary gifts" without asking their consent. In a century like Newman's, when priesthood is considered "a livelihood" that involved "a comparatively easy" life, one which supplied "respectability and comfort" along with "a position in society," this ancient practice must have seemed strange and unnatural. Third, there were "national conversions" during the middle ages, when "kings submitted to the Gospel" and their subjects followed them. Whether this was well or ill advised, it happened, and the action was accompanied with "state penalties" for those who "promulgated any heterodox tenet."

Until now, the sermon has described and discussed the "law of Providence" in which compulsion is essential, but before it concludes the sermon has a surprise in store. In the three sections so far reviewed, the degree of nearness to the audience has gone from the remote of hypothetical and parable, to the proximate in the remarks upon Christian baptism and education, then back again in the third section to the remoteness of the historical reflection on medieval compulsion. Then suddenly, the fourth section lunges into the laps of its readers, so to speak, to fervently advocate bringing the young to confirmation before it is too late. Those who leave childhood no longer enjoy its "privilege and mercy of being dependent," and just as they are about to reach adult status, the Church "blesses them by force and lets them go." Newman adjures those who have the care of adolescents, "let not the time slip by; let them not get too old," since then you cannot bring them for the Church's blessing, which "conveys to them grace" to perform the work baptism has begun. The surprise in the sermon is the sense of urgency which overtakes the audience. If a grown person comes "coldly, and indifferently" to be confirmed, it is too late, so do not "let slip the time." On the other hand if you are a young person (here Newman shifts into direct address), be confirmed now, for "you cannot trust your own promises about yourself." You must receive the gifts of grace when they are offered. "They are, as it were, forced upon you now"; comply, for "the season once lost will never return." If you neglect God's loving compulsion, you may be about to enter the state of "slavery to the world."

The other member of the first sermon pair, "Reliance on Religious Observances," imposes order on a subject murky enough in itself to resist clarification, which is commonly the case with amorphous charges of moral turpitude levelled against others. The subject is self-righteousness, and the charge Newman examines is that the religious engagements of observant Christians tend to make them self-satisfied. The sermon's epigraph is the text from Luke, "When ye shall have done all those things which are commanded you, say, We are unprofitable servants." Opening the introductory section, Newman says that "if *reason* is to be judge," there can be "no boasting toward God" because all we do is "the fruit of His grace," we do very little, that little is "infected with sin," and even if we did all, it would only be what is expected of us. Following this brief analysis of the Christian's situation, Newman inserts an objection, one that will spur him into counterargument: "And yet, it will be said, there are many persons in the world who are well-pleased with what they are and what they do," i.e., persons who are commonly called self-righteous. What merit is there in this charge? Newman responds with the counter-assertions, first, that self-righteous persons are those who "live to the world, and do not think of God," second, that such persons live in the "visible and tangible, and do not measure themselves by what is unseen and spiritual," and third, that they "measure themselves merely by their own conscience," which is "dark and blind." Looked at another way, the self-righteous typically "fasten their minds" upon some religious object that is "short of God," thus narrowing the field of duty, and thereafter use that contracted rule to measure their performance. This is a procedure easily fallen into, for the "vivid consciousness" they have of the narrowed object they pursue persuades them that they "act up to it." But again, as Newman reminds his readers, no one can consider himself "meritorious" in God's sight who thinks seriously about the matter. This is "the real state of the case."

Newman next advances another version of the accusation which was considered earlier: "However, the popular view of spiritual pride or self-righteousness is this, that those men are self-righteous, or in danger of being so, who come often to Church, and are diligent in their moral duties." Having articulated the position which he will reject, the preacher says "let us then consider, from this hint given us by ignorant and prejudiced men," whether the Christian, blessed with the privileges of prayer and Holy Communion, is "in any special danger of spiritual pride." The first phase of his answer, which is relatively brief, is that indeed such cases are possible, particularly because "what is contained in definite outward acts has a completeness and tangible form about it, which is likely to *satisfy* the mind." However, that possibility is no "very great danger to a serious mind," since Christ's gifts are mercies, not snares. Having dealt with this possibility, Newman shifts into his central argument: "Let us then see how the danger of self-righteousness is counteracted," which he does in three movements. First, self-righteousness can injure us only "when we do not know its existence," since knowing we are self-satisfied "is a direct blow to self-satisfaction." The operative principle here is that evil thoughts cannot harm us if we recognize and protest against them "by the indignation and self-reproach of the mind." Second, when religious persons have thoughts about "their own excellence and strictness," it generally occurs when they are "young in their religion," and is a trial that will "wear off" as they widen their perception to include the whole field of duty before them. The principle is that the narrower the field of our duties, the better able we are "to compass them," while broadening the field has the humbling opposite effect. Third, the objection that prayer, fasting, and the like tend towards self-righteousness "is the objection, or at least is what the objection of those would be, who never attempted them," as if it were "the easiest thing in the world to fast and pray." Newman answers this uninformed notion with the *argumentum* based upon personal experience.

> Is it an easy thing to pray? It *is* easy to wait for a rush of feelings, and then to let our petitions be borne upon them . . . But it is not at all easy to be in the habit day after day and hour after hour, in all frames of mind, and under all outward circumstances, to bring before God a calm, collected, awakened soul . . . Where is the really serious mind that will say it is easy to take delight in stated prayer, to attend to it duly? Is not at the best our delight in it transient, and our attention irregular? Is all this satisfactory and elating? 4.75–6

The same may be said about austerities, although there are people so constituted that they seem to enjoy mortification for its own sake. Concluding that portion of his argument, Newman insists that surely it is "idle to speak of this as an ordinary danger," for such is emphatically not the case.

The last stage of the sermon, instead of being another group of arguments brought against the views of those who wrongly accuse prayerful Christians of self-righteousness, consists of the consolatory conclusion phase, the spirit-lifting send-off announced by the rhetorical question "But, after all, what is this shrinking from responsibility, which fears to be obedient lest it should fail, but cowardice and ingratitude?" Newman does not attribute such cowardice to his audience. Quite the contrary, because he knows they will be *with him* when he says "to fear to do our duty lest we should become self-righteous in doing so, is to be wiser than God." It would be "to do and feel like the unprofitable servant who hid his Lord's talent, and then laid the charge of his sloth on his Lord, as being a hard and austere man," an allusion which binds together the two sermons of the initial pair. If one did not know that the first of these sermons was written or first preached in March, 1835, the second in April, 1837, and the volume they appear together in not assembled until November, 1838, one could imagine that the connective allusion was deliberately intended. But, that dating being decisive, the allusion in the second sermon to the epigraph of the first must be seen as a fortunate coincidence, made possible by the thematic consanguinity of the two.

In retrospect, the first pair of sermons persuades by argument, whether positive or negative. That is, the first sermon brings evidence to demonstrate that compulsion is an inevitable aspect of Providence, while the second disproves the false charge that religious observances tend to make Christians self-righteous. However, the second pair pursue a quite different method, because while they too hope to persuade, their strategy is not argument but meditative reflection. These two sermons both rely upon a method one might call assisted self-reflection: the preacher energizes the auditor, who already in part knows or intuits certain aspects of spiritual reality, in order to help him more deeply burrow-into that experience and draw-out more of it into full awareness. If argument is external in the sense that it resides in the case which is made on the basis of objective evidence, then by contrast meditative reflection is more internal, the evidence brought being subjective perceptions which are not the fruit of demonstration, but of elicitation. The auditor is in this procedure more correctly described as a participating coadjutor than as the evaluator of a case being argued.

"The Invisible World" hinges upon the tension between sight and faith since the world that we see appears already to occupy and exhaust the space which any other world would need in order to exist. The sermon's epigraph, St. Paul's statement to the Corinthians "the things which are seen are temporal, but the things which are not seen are eternal," raises the question, where might the things which are not seen exist, if they be real? That is the difficulty Newman addresses, his position being that the eternal world "really exists, though we see it not," and it exists here among us now. He begins with a visual survey of the world into which we are born, celebrating its great variety and majestic scope as the prelude to discussing the co-presence of the invisible domain.

> All that meets our eyes forms one world. It is an immense world; it reaches to the stars. Thousands on thousands of years might we speed up the sky, and though we were swifter than the light itself, we should not reach them all. They are at distances from us greater than any that is assignable. So high, so wide, so deep is the world; and yet it also comes near and close to us. It is every where; and it seems to leave no room for any other world.
>
> And yet in spite of this universal world we see, there is another world, quite as far-spreading, quite as close to us, and more wonderful; another world, all around us, though we see it not, and more wonderful than the world we see, for this reason if for no other, that we do not see it. All around us are numberless objects, coming and going, watching, working or waiting, which we see not; this is that other world, which the eyes reach not unto, but faith only. 4.200–1

This is not argument, but rather a lyrical exploration which advances by juxtaposition: the visible world "reaches to the stars," so remote from us that, were we faster than the speed of light, we could never "reach them all," yet here among us is "that other world, which the eyes reach not unto, but faith only." To dwell upon this thought, as Newman invites his readers to do, is to meditate upon the strangeness of the double universe which we inhabit, in which our familiar visible world "does not interfere with the existence of that other world," which acts upon us without our being conscious of it. "Almighty God" exists there, as well the souls of the dead, who live as they lived before though they no longer "act towards us" through our senses. Angels inhabit this invisible world, which we know from Jacob's vision of a ladder connecting earth and heaven, which had "angels ascending and descending thereon, And behold, the Lord stood above it." Newman observes that people "commonly speak as if the other world did not exist now, but would after death." Yet it "exists now, though we see it not." What Jacob saw in his dream the shepherds at the Nativity both saw and heard. Evidently, then, we exist "in a world of spirits, as well as in a world of sense."

Having proceeded thus far on the original impetus that the epigraph provided him, Newman adverts once again to the same passage from *II Corinthians*, observing that St. Paul "regarded it as a practical truth" that we are to look at the invisible world, and that their belonging to time is "a reason, not for looking at, but for looking off" temporal things. It is the only practical course for Christians to follow, because the invisible kingdom of God, "as it is now hidden, so in due season shall it be revealed." Here is the transition statement that redirects the sermon from its initial expository section to its concluding celebration of the things which are to be revealed "in due season." Then, "this world will fade away and the other world will shine forth."

> Let these be your thoughts my brethren, expecially in the spring season, when the whole face of nature is so rich and beautiful. Once only in the year, yet once, does the world which we see show forth its hidden powers, and in a manner manifest itself. Then the leaves come out, and the blossoms on the fruit trees and flowers; and the grass and corn spring up. There is a sudden rush and burst outwardly of that hidden life which God has lodged in the material world. 4.209

Briefly interrupting this lyric celebration of spring, Newman points out its significance for his audience: "Well, that shows you, as by a sample, what [the earth] can do at God's command, when He gives the word." Articulating the analogy very baldly, he continues "This earth, which now buds forth in leaves and blossoms, will one day burst forth into a new world of light and glory, in which, we shall see Saints and Angels dwelling." The surprise will be as great as when, after a delayed spring, the "naked branches" of the trees are suddenly clothed with living color. As this celebration of the unseen world proceeds, Newman punctuates it with intermittent direct address to God.

> So it is with the coming of the Eternal Spring, for which all Christians are waiting. Come it will, though it delay . . . Therefore we say day by day, "Thy kingdom come;" which means,—O Lord, show Thyself; manifest Thyself; Thou that sittest between the Cherubim, show Thyself; stir up Thy strength and come and help us. The earth that we see does not satisfy us; it is but a beginning; it is but a promise of something beyond it; even when it is gayest, with all its blossoms on, and shows most touchingly what lies hid in it, yet it is not enough. We know much more lies hid in it than we see. A world of Saints and Angels, a glorious world, a palace of God, the mountain of the Lord of Hosts, the heavenly Jerusalem, the throne of God and Christ, all these wonders, everlasting, all-precious, mysterious, and incomprehensible, lie hid in what we see. What we see is the outward shell of an eternal kingdom; and on that kingdom we fix the eyes of our faith. Shine forth, O Lord, as when on Thy Nativity Thine Angels visited the shepherds; let Thy glory blossom forth as bloom and foliage on the trees; change with Thy mighty power this visible world into that diviner world, which as yet we see not; destroy what we see, that it may pass and be transformed into what we believe. 4.210–11

Closing out the sermon, Newman reflects briefly on the rapture those will feel "who shall at length behold what as yet mortal eye hath not seen and faith only enjoys," that first "waking from the dead" when, "after long rest," we find ourselves "vigorous with the seed of eternal life within us." How to set this high-flying lyrical paean back on the earth? "Earthly words are indeed all but worthless" to express such "high anticipations," and therefore Newman, for closure, cuts away to the relevant passage from *Isaiah* (40:6–8): "The grass withereth, the flower fadeth; but the Word of our God shall stand for ever."

While "The Invisible World" explores the cosmology of faith, "The Greatness and Littleness of Human Life" is a meditation upon the common human perception of the mismatch between our spiritual powers and the inadequate time which human existence allows for their expression. The epigraph is Jacob's lamentation, when one hundred and thirty years old, "few and evil have the days of my life been." Newman anticipates the objection that Jacob's days were many, and his life hardly evil since he enjoyed riches and honor. He answers it by observing that the longest life is short, the grandest achievements empty once they have passed. This is a thought which occasionally comes upon us, he states, "and many perhaps" who think they have never felt that way "may recognize what I mean" when they hear it described. Newman is hoping to elicit from his audience an explicit awareness of something which they, in some sense, already understand. The reason life can seem brief and unfulfilling is that "we see implied in it the presence of a soul, of an accountable being." Yet when we look back in memory we conceive of it "externally, as a mere lapse of time," and the longest span of chronological time "weighs nothing, against one moment's life of the world within." Moreover, life is always giving promises but seldom fulfillment, which is why it would seem that our days are "few and evil." That is the "particular view" of the subject Newman intends to dwell upon, with his attentively engaged audience.

Newman begins to dwell upon that thought by inviting his auditors to recollect some person they knew, admirable in some respect or other, who lived out his days and died, surprising them with the feeling that he had left the world too soon, having had insufficient scope for his "excellent gifts," not having spent the "treasure within him." After that, the preacher elicits a further meditation, this time upon a friend whose life has been cut short—Hurrel Froude comes to mind, although Newman does not mention his greatly gifted friend who died a tragically early death. Everybody can supply a personal instance of such a loss. "They are suddenly taken away, and we have hardly recognized them when we lose them." Have they not been "removed for higher things elsewhere?" we may ask ourselves. This sentiment is provoked not by intellectual gifts alone, because there is "something in faith, in firmness, in heavenly-mindedness, in meekness, in courage, in loving-kindness, to which this world's circumstances are quite unequal, for which the longest life is insufficient, which makes the highest opportunities of this world disappointing, which must burst the prison of this world to have its appropriate range." One recognizes that the lamentation over human potential unfulfilled has been gradually coming around towards a very different sort of predication: an inference that the limits imposed by mortality should not occasion stoical endurance, but instead should give rise to the recognition that those limits are the walls of a "prison" destined to be "burst" open, freeing those locked within. That is the point which Newman's meditation on temporality has hoped to elicit from his audience.

> Unless our faith be very active, so as to pierce beyond the grave, and realize the future, we feel depressed at what seems like a failure of great things. And from this very feeling surely, by a sort of contradiction, we may fairly take hope; for if this life be so disappointing, so unfinished, surely it is not the whole. 4.219

Newman proceeds beyond this juncture by imagining the emotion which could be thought to come over "the soul of the faithful Christian" when just separated from the body, now aware that his trial is finally ended. It is a feeling such as is provoked by suddenly finding a much anticipated opportunity or trial, one for which we have "wound up our minds," finished, behind us. We undergo "a strange reverse of feeling" because of our changed circumstances, and most of all we feel a contentment born of relief at having stood the test. "What an easy trial," we may think to ourselves. And this response is perhaps succeeded by the reflection, "How contemptible a thing," in itself, is human life. But on the other hand, we see it is of inestimable value since we have found it to be "like a small seed of easy purchase, germinating and ripening into bliss everlasting." What insight has "The Greatness and Littleness of Human Life" elicited from its audience? Only they can say, of course. However, it is clear that the preacher's intention has been "to lead us to rejoice in every day and hour that passes, as bringing us nearer the time of [Christ's] appearing, and the termination of sin and misery."

The third sermon pair, "Christ Hidden from the World" and "Christ Manifested in Remembrance," is about spiritual perception. Though Jesus and the Holy Ghost continue to be present in the world, our realization of that fact hinges upon the reflective perception which these sermons explore. Newman's rhetorical strategy is argument, not elicitation, because once again he brings evidence to construct a case, this time to clarify how Christians can recognize Christ's presence. "Christ Hidden from the World" points out that, as in his earthly life "many saw" but "few indeed discerned Him," so is the case true today. Jesus is still among us, but not to the perceptions of those blinded by unbelief. The argument is divided into four stages, the first being an analysis of the secrecy in which Jesus concealed Himself before His Ascension. Born of a poor woman in a provincial town, raised under the protective cover of obscurity, for thirty years hidden in the crowds, He remained unrecognized even by his closest relatives; when He began to preach they "went out to lay hold of Him," supposing He had gone mad, for though they had long lived with Him, they did not know Him. By thus putting together fragments of evidence which the Gospels contain, Newman elaborates the epigraph which provides the theme for his sermonic invention: "The light shineth in darkness; and the darkness comprehended it not."

The next phase of the sermon begins with the assertion that Christ might now be our next door neighbor and we "not find it out," a thought "that should be dwelt on." We live among many sorts of people, from open sinners to secretly holy persons, who all "look about the same" to us——which is no surprise because genuine religion is "a hidden life in the heart." Nevertheless, a really holy man "has a sort of secret power in him to attract others to him who are like-minded," and thus "it often becomes a test, whether we are like-minded" with the saintly among us, "whether they have an influence over us." The holier a man, "the less he is understood by the world," which is what "happened to our Lord." It remains still true what was true then, the light shined but the darkness failed to notice. Therefore, "it surely becomes a question whether we should have understood Him better than" Christ's contemporaries did. Here is a potentially disconcerting thought, says Newman, because "if He were near us for a long time" and we not sensible of it, such blindness could be taken as "clear proof that we were not His," because His sheep know His voice and follow Him.

The sermon's third phase begins with this conditional: we are apt to think that we would have lived better lives in Christ's immediate presence. But as Newman reflects, "so far from our sinful habits being reformed" by nearness to the Lord, it is more likely that those habits would have "hindered us from recognizing Him," such that, had He told us who He was, we would not have believed. The evidence is this, that the Roman torturers, those who seized, stripped, scourged and spit upon Christ before stretching Him on the cross and nailing Him to it, came as near to Him as human beings can, and yet they "knew nothing about it," having no senses to guide them, any more than have the cattle milling about the shambles, Newman says, who ignorantly sniff the instruments of their own slaughter.

The fourth and last movement of the sermon begins with the question, "But you may say, how does this concern us? Christ is not here; we cannot thus or in any less way insult His Majesty." But are we so sure of this? Greater sins than those of Jesus' executioners are possible, though not "so flagrant or open." If Christ be still on earth yet not visibly so, then He maintains the condition He chose at first, and "whatever be the tokens of His Presence," they must be ambiguous enough that they allow people to doubt where He is. Indeed, it is probable that those tokens are "of a nature easily to lead men into irreverence" if they are not humble and watchful. Newman offers his readers an illustrative example of how easy it is for the irreverent to mistake his presence.

> The Church is called "His Body:" what His material Body was when He was visible on earth, such is the Church now. It is the instrument of His Divine power; it is that which we must approach, to gain good from Him; it is that which by insulting we awaken His anger. Now, what is the Church but, as it were, a body of humiliation, almost provoking insult and profaneness, when we do not live by faith? 4.250

Similarly, the poor, the weak and afflicted are "tokens and instruments" of His presence, and here too we find the same temptation "to neglect or profane it." When Jesus said "I was thirsty, and ye gave Me drink," the response which he rhetorically assigns to compassionate persons who tended to His needs unknowingly is surprise. Those who neglected to help the helpless reacted with surprise as well, for, says Newman, "neither righteous nor wicked *knew* what they had done," and what was the case then remains true today. In every age, "Christ is both in the world, and yet not publicly so more than in the days of His flesh."

The epigraph of "Christ Manifested in Remembrance" is the risen Savior's promise to His disciples that He would send the Spirit as a Comforter, and "He shall glorify Me." The sermon points out that glorification is "more real" to the degree that it is the "more secret and inscrutable." Newman first considers how the Holy Spirit gives glory to Christ, then inquires whether there be in that transaction "some trace of a general law of Providence" that holds true not only in Scripture, but in "the world's affairs." While its companion's strategy is to present evidence in support of a conclusion, this sermon does so only in part, since it depends very heavily on the audience's personal experience, reflection upon that being their contribution to the mutual effort required by the sermon.

The Holy Ghost gives glory to the Son by revealing Him more completely, because while Christ "declared the whole truth," his followers understood it only in part because Jesus "purposely concealed" the truth which he spoke, as if "reserving" to the Spirit its complete disclosure. Only after the Holy Ghost's descent did the Apostles realize who Jesus was. "When all was over they knew it, not at the time"; that is the general principle the sermon elucidates. "God's presence is not discerned at the time when it is upon us, but afterwards, when we look back on what is gone and over."

The Scriptural instances of the general principle that the sermon offers include Jesus' query "Have I been so long time with you, and yet hast thou not known me, Philip?" Then to Peter, when Christ was about to wash his Apostles' feet, "What I do thou knowest not now, but thou shalt know hereafter." And finally, the emotion felt by the disciples walking to Emmaus, who did not at first recognize Him, but later exclaimed "Did not our hearts burn within us" when the risen Savior opened the scriptures to them. Parallel instances of this principle are found in the Old Testament as well: Jacob's not realizing until he awoke from sleep that "Surely the Lord is in this place, and I knew it not"; Gideon's discovering what had occurred only after the angel had departed; and Manoah's observation to his wife once the angel had left them, "we shall surely die, because we have seen God." All these instances exemplify the general rule Newman is exploring, that what occurred is not known when it happens, but is grasped "by faith, afterwards only."

The second part of the exposition, which shows how the principle operates in "the providences of daily life," elicits from the audience the same sorts of experiences as those recorded in Scripture. Indeed, Newman returns to the Old Testament to find precisely such experiences, above all Jacob's crying out "all these things are against me"—Joseph dead, Simeon in prison in Egypt, Benjamin about to be taken from him—misfortunes in which the devastated father cannot recognize these disasters as the means by which the family is delivered from the famine. As Joseph tells his brothers later, "It was not you that sent me hither, but God." In like manner, Newman says, let anyone who on the whole is serving God "look back upon his past life, and he will find how critical were moments and acts, which at the time seemed the most indifferent," like the school he attended, his friendships with those whose influence most benefitted him, and those accidents which determined "his calling or prospects." On the basis of their own experience, Newman suggests, his audience will appreciate God's leading us on by ways we "cannot see now."

Childhood, too, frequently remembered as having been "bright and glorious," commonly raises affectionate feeling without those who recall the time knowing quite why. "They think it is those very years which they yearn after," but as they later see, it is God's presence which was upon them in that period, which attracts them. "They think that they regret the past, when they are but longing for the future." What happens in personal lives happens also in the life of the Church when times of persecution end. Those who seemed to direct the world, the great men

> who in their day so magnified themselves, so ravaged and deformed the Church, that it could not be seen except by faith, then are found in nowise to have infringed the continuity of its outlines, which shine out clear and glorious, and even more delicate and tender for the very attempt to obliterate them. It needs very little study of history to prove how really this is the case; how little schism and divisions and disorders and troubles and fears and persecutions and scatterings and threatenings interfere with the glory of Christ Mystical, as looked upon afterwards, though at the time they almost hid it. Great Saints, great events, great privileges, like the everlasting mountains, grow as we recede from them. 4.263

Even our individual experience of the Church's sacraments follows the pattern Newman is presenting. During periods of sickness, agitation and restlessness which at the moment distract us, we cannot understand that "Christ is with us." In such periods, we come in darkness to lie down like Jacob with a stone for our pillow. But in retrospect "we are led to cry out, 'This is *none other* than the house of God, and this is the gate of heaven.'"

The fourth sermon pair, "Watching" and "Keeping Fast and Festival," focuses on the Christian's challenge to live in time without neglecting to serve Christ with a generous heart. In the epigraphs of these sermons the verbs "watch" and "keep" name both the difficulty and the opportunity of turning our ordinary religious observances into an enduring allegiance to Christ, one which becomes the permanent form of our souls. The best preparation for understanding these sermons rightly is to reflect on St. Augustine's definition of time, for he and Newman share the same conception of its nature, conceiving it not as a measure of external change such as continental drift or the dispersion of gasses, but instead as a spiritual dimension, that within which we live and move and have our religious being.

In Book 11 of his *Confessions*, Augustine dismisses two erroneous views: that the movements of the sun, moon and stars constitute time (23:29); and that time consists of past, present and future. However, as Augustine continues,

> it might properly be said that there are three times, the present of things past, the present of things present, and the present of things future. These three are in the soul, but elsewhere I do not see them: the present of things past is in memory; the present of things present is in intuition; the present of things future is in expectation. 20:26

If that be true, what is time? "Time is nothing more than distention: but of what thing I know not, and the marvel is, if it be not of the mind itself" (26:33). In a helpful explanatory note, John K. Ryan, the translator of this English version of the *Confessions*, clarifies the term distention (*distentio*) by saying that for Augustine time is

> an activity of the mind, whereby the mind is not merely extended into the past, as in memory, or into the future, as in anticipation, but is distended, so as to hold things as present. 411, note 2

That is also the essence of Newman's understanding of time: it is a mental activity, one wherein the mind is distended, stretched, told to reach backwards and forwards, "so as to hold things as present." Newman's "watching" and "keeping" are versions of this activity.

The epigraph of "Watching," which is "Watch and pray, for ye know not when the time is," orients us towards an indefinite moment so important that it must be kept ever in mind. This is difficult, yet no more than Jesus and His Apostles demand. The sermon's strategy is dependent on the constant reiteration of the identical message, through the unseemly multiplication of Scriptural quotations. Thus for example, Jesus says "if the goodman of the house had known what hour the thief would come, he would have *watched*," He narrates the parable of the Wise and Foolish Virgins, and He asks Peter "couldst not thou *watch* one hour?" The Apostles, too, repetitively insist upon the same message, Paul saying "*watch* ye, stand fast in the faith," and Peter, "be *vigilant*, because your adversary the devil, as a roaring lion," and John, "Behold I come as a thief; blessed is he that *watcheth*." Knowing that repetition dulls the minds of audiences, and that that which is too often heard is ignored, Newman, paradoxically, serves them an overload of such quotations as if to awaken interest by the force of conspicuous redundancy. He follows the insistence of such reduplicative quotation by observing that the word watching is "a remarkable word" for two reasons: because the idea it conveys "is not so obvious as might appear at first sight," and because Christ and His Apostles "all inculcate it." The Christian is not only to believe, to love, and to obey, but to watch for Christ's coming. Watching, the mobilizing of our attention to anticipate and expect that event, is "a special duty enjoined on us," not one that would come into our minds naturally.

Moving to the sermon's next stage, Newman asks "What is watching?" and then gives a series of further rhetorical questions aimed at eliciting from his audience their lively recollection of natural watching, i.e., preoccupation with a future moment anticipated with a certain emotional force.

> Do you know the feeling of expecting a friend, expecting him to come and he delays? Do you know what it is to be in unpleasant company, and to wish for the time to pass away, and the hour to strike when you may be at liberty? Do you know what it is to be in anxiety lest something should happen or not, or to be in suspense about some important event, which makes your heart beat when you are reminded of it, and of which you think the first thing in the morning? 4.322–3

Drawing out the parallel explicitly, Newman says "To watch for Christ is a feeling such as all of these; as far as feelings of this world are fit to shadow out those of another."

Having described the characteristic emotional tone of Christian watching, Newman distinguishes two levels of that activity: watching "*for*" Christ, and watching "*with*" Him. He watches for Christ who is "quick-sighted" in seeking Him and "would not be surprised" at His immediate return. On the other hand "he watches *with* Christ, who, while he looks on to the future, looks back on the past, and does not so contemplate what his Saviour has purchased for him, as to forget what He suffered." He watches with Christ "who ever commemorates and renews in his own person Christ's Cross and Agony." For that person time, as Augustine understands it, is distended so as to hold things past and expectations of the future as realities "present" within the soul.

> This then is to watch; to be detached from what is present, and to live in what is unseen; to live in the thought of Christ as He came once, and as He will come again; to desire His second coming, from our affectionate and grateful remembrance of His first. And this it is, in which we shall find that men in general are wanting. 4.325

The quotation's closing sentence marks the shift from Newman's operational definition of watching with Christ, to his analysis of how most Christians avoid that obligation. The generality of Christians "have no definite idea" what watching means or how it could be their duty. They are not bad men, revilers of religion, but are "of a more sober and conscientious cast of mind." Yet they fail to understand that they are "called to be strangers and pilgrims upon the earth." Though they have many excellent qualities, their temper of mind is essentially earthly. "They may improve in conduct, but not in aims; they advance, but they do not mount," and even if they lived for centuries they would never "rise above the atmosphere of this world." The mirror within them, their soul, having been rusted by the breath of the world, is now "dim and discoloured." So far, the distancing pronoun "they" has shielded Newman's readers from his accusations. But before he finishes, the preacher brings the charges closer to home by shifting into the more intimate, more audience-near pronoun "we." Newman says "we deceive our better judgment" and by doing so become "over-anxious, fretful, and care-worn about worldly matters." By such failures "we take our portion with this world," though we "obstinately refuse" to believe that we do, for we know we are "not altogether irreligious," and at last "learn to think it possible to be too religious."

Thus we are not "standing like soldiers on the watch in the dark night; but we kindle our own fire, and delight ourselves in the sparks of it." Here is a representative piece of Newman's rhetoric, one which does not dissipate its energy upon "diction, elocution" and the like, since it is all matter, no art. In brief space, the preacher likens the religious betrayal of proudly preferring the "sparks of our own fire" to God's creative fiat "Let there be light," and combines that failure of allegiance with Peter's denial when accused by the servant girl (before the high priest's palace while huddling around the fire to warm himself) of being Christ's companion.

After employing the accusation-useful personal pronoun "we" to bring closer to home the sermon's reflections upon Christians' real defection from their ostensible allegiance to Christ, Newman discontinues that rhetorical strategy and offers his hearers encouragement in the good fight. As the sermon moves to its conclusion, it echoes something of the lyrical splendor of "The Invisible World" we saw earlier in Volume 4. Here too, he reminds his audience that Christ is not far off though He seems to be, but close behind this visible screen of things which hides Him from us. He is behind this material framework; earth and sky are but a veil going between Him and us; the day will come when He will rend that veil, and reveal Himself to us. The sermon tells us prepare to meet Him *then* by watching *with* Him now.

The key word in the title "Keeping Fast and Festival" is keeping, which signifies observing, remembering, showing appropriate regard for, as one would keep one's promise or treasure a keepsake because of a relationship of obligation to another. The title refers to the duty of observing the Holy Days in the Church's calendar, the liturgical year in which Christ's life and sacrificial death are commemorated. The Christian has a relationship of obligation to Him, and keeping fast and festival are one way of honoring the bond of love. The epigraph, "A time to weep, a time to laugh; a time to mourn, a time to dance," which would seem meant to introduce a survey of the fluctuating emotional tonality of the Church year, announces an Easter sermon focused on the disparity between the mournful spirit of Lent and the joy of Christ's Resurrection. The epigraph's "time to dance" is difficult to realize on Easter because the rigors of the Lenten season do not easily give way to elation. The joy of Easter is sober and resigned, "a last feeling and not a first," says Newman. He finds the emotion appropriate for the season not a single feeling, but a blending of several conflicting states of mind within a continuing process of soul transformation. St. Paul says it well: "Tribulation worketh patience, and patience experience, and experience hope; and hope maketh not ashamed." As the *Jerusalem Bible* states it, "this hope is not deceptive" but can be depended on since "the love of God is shed abroad in our hearts." However, this frame of mind—the goal of our transformation in Christ—is the final stage of a gruelling journey.

The rhetorical strategy of "Keeping Fast and Festival" is not argument, neither is it elicitation, since Newman's experience rather than the reader's is being reflected on. Its strategy can better be defined as heightened contrast, which is also seen in the first member of this sermon pair. For example, watching is so demanding that "men in general" have "no definite idea" what it means or how it could be a duty, for the breath of the world has "rusted" their souls. The juxtaposition between the spiritual transformation St. Paul describes and living with a "rusted" soul exemplifies the rhetorical tool of the heightened contrast. Similarly, in "Keeping Fast and Festival" the emotional debility that results from fervent commemoration of Christ's Agony makes it impossible to experience the joy appropriate for Easter; this stands in contrast to the *absence* of religious emotion in "the world at large." Many Christians "do not realize the next world at all," for they "do not make our Saviour's life and death present to them." Having thought that they could "dispense with the religious Ordinances" included in the "Sacred Seasons of the Church," they lose the rewards of fervent participation. Newman contrasts their defection from ideals to which they extend a nominal adherence, with the Apostles' better example. Following the Resurrection, Christ's friends experienced the "pensive and tender and joyful melancholy" of those who "have gone through pain" so recently that elation is not within their grasp. Such was Mary Magdalen, weeping at the tomb, then embracing Christ's feet. So, too, were Peter and the others on the seashore, quietly eating of the fish, until Jesus "broke silence by asking Peter if he loved Him." Newman concludes the sermon by advising his audience to work for the Kingdom as did the Apostles because the transformation begun in us by baptism can only proceed through our active engagement, "as we are made His continually, by the recurring celebration of his purifying Fasts and Holy Feasts."

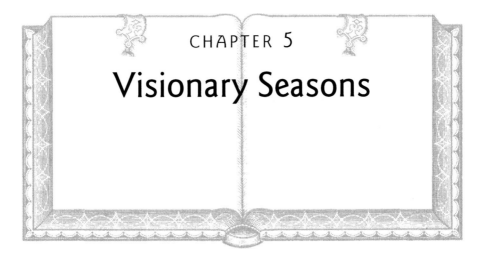

CHAPTER 5

Visionary Seasons

Although they were published two years apart in 1840 and 1842, the concluding volumes of *Parochial Sermons* are designed as the two halves of a compositional whole that meditates upon the liturgical seasons of the Church year. In Volume 2, Newman had squeezed the entire *Book of Common Prayer*'s Table of Holy Days into the constricted space of 32 sermons, which caused certain problems. Most notably, doing so forced him to constantly alternate between Feast Days celebrating doctrinal truths and Saints' Days honoring the Apostles' actions, which robbed him of the opportunity for the massing of thematically related adjacent sermons. Experience having taught him to manage differently his second attempt to traverse the Church calendar, Newman organized the 49 sermons of Volumes 5 and 6 on the basis of liturgical *seasons* rather than individual feasts, a plan which lends itself to a more concentrated yet at the same time more varied series of meditations on the devotional attitudes called forth by those seasons (Lams 2004, 87). Volume 5 covers the liturgical times of Advent, Christmas, and Epiphany, followed by a pre-Lenten season that Newman generates by expanding the three Sundays before Lent into the reflective space of seven sermons, thus ending the 24 sermon volume at just the point, Lent, where the 25 sermons of Volume 6 begin. These changes in volume organization enhance the gradual and sustained assimilation of seasonal significance—the focus being no longer on the corruptions of Christian doctrine, as in some earlier volumes. Now, reflection on doctrinal error operates as a con-

trast device rather than a tocsin call to theological reform. Overall, the tone of
Volumes 5 and 6 is patiently positive.

"Seasons" in the title indicates the generic subject of these concluding volumes,
while "visionary" reminds us of the distinctive quality of the collection as a georgic. As previously defined, the visionary georgic focuses upon a central truth presented as essential to the spiritual well-being of the audience, and the Introduction
identifies its two modes, the Mirror and the Lamp. It happens that these two cor-
respond to Aristotle's twin modes of rhetoric, i.e., argument based upon things
which are already there, such as contracts and witnesses, and those based upon
things which do not yet exist and thus have to be invented. The mirror georgicists
Lucretius and Newman both rely upon witnesses, Epicurus and Divine Revelation,
though both authors need to invent arguments which apply their witnesses' testimony to their own georgic intentions. But Wordsworth, being a lamp georgicist,
invents The Prelude out of whole cloth, for he is his own witness. Everything he has
to say comes from his personal experience of the relations between external physical nature and the perceptions and emotions generated by his reflective sensibility.

Wordsworth was a nominal Anglican who knew the plot forms and vocabulary of Christianity, but whose interest had crossed the divide separating religion
from literature. His poetry uses the forms of Christian faith to articulate his romantic celebration of self and nature. This is clear in his early lyric "A Night Piece,"
which contains in small the gist of his fourteen-book Prelude. In the earlier poem
Wordsworth presents us with a "pensive traveller" who is a naturalized Bunyan-style
pilgrim walking his path, his eyes earthward underneath "a continuous cloud of texture close,/ Heavy and wan, all whitened by the Moon," indistinctly seen "through
that veil." The cloud-cover veil is a naturalized version of Scripture's veil overshad-
owing the nations and separating them from God. Startled by a sudden gleam from
on high, Wordsworth's traveller "looks up," and in doing so has a revelatory visual experience: the clouds are "split/ Asunder,—and above his head he sees/ The
clear Moon, and the glory of the heavens." Though the vision soon closes, the
mind, "Not undisturbed by the delight it feels" (which resembles the elation of the
disciples who recognize Christ on the road to Emmaus), draws sustenance from "the
solemn scene" which has just closed.

The main difference between this 26 line lyric written in 1798 and the
fourteen-book Prelude, first published in its final form in 1850, is the later poem's
greater length and fuller elaboration of the nutshell version found in "A Night
Piece," because the climactic night-ascent of Mount Snowden in Book 14 of The
Prelude repeats the same pattern: the revelatory sense experience generates self-
exploratory reflection. When "in calm thought" Wordsworth muses upon the
bright vision of the Moon presiding majestically over the sea of fog, through which
the hills lift up their backs like primeval beasts cavorting in the ocean of time, it

appears to him "the type of a majestic intellect, its acts . . . / What in itself it is, and would become" (XIV.66–9). The power that is felt by "bodily sense" is the correlative of the "glorious faculty that higher minds bear with them as their own" (XIV. 88–9). Wordsworth is the solitary soul communing with the soul of nature, the "higher mind" being celebrated, the "majestic intellect" often projected into the deistic space of physico-theology, but here taken to be the glory of the poet's intellectual power. *The Prelude's* climax is Wordsworth's naturalized religious ascension to glory upon the mountain top, his transfiguration there.

What Keats as a sensitive reader could not help but see and characterize in Wordsworth as "the wordsworthian or egotistical sublime," Newman, a professional critic of the forms taken by such degenerative Christianity, describes at greater length in a sermon we have already examined, i.e., "Self-Contemplation." Therein, Newman says this about the condition experienced by the nominal Christian Wordsworth:

> The last and most miserable stage of this false wisdom is, to deny that in matters of doctrine there is any one sense of Scripture such, that it is true and all others false. [The effect of this] is to throw us back into the vagueness of Heathenism, where men only felt after the Divine Presence. [Such persons] lay all the stress upon the direct creation, in their minds, of faith and spiritual-mindedness, which they consider to consist in certain emotions and desires. [As a result,] a sort of self-approbation will insinuate itself into the mind: so subtle as not at once to be recognized by himself,—-an habitual quiet self-esteem, leading him to prefer his own views to those of others, and a secret, if not avowed persuasion, that he is in a different state from the generality of those around him. 2.167–8,171

Like Newman a mirror georgicist, Lucretius begins with the testimony of Epicurus regarding matter, space, atoms, void and the infinite, these being the key concepts in the Greek thinker's physics that the Roman poet adopted. F. O. Copley summarizes Epicurus' philosophy, the part of it that Lucretius presented for his audience: our senses reveal a material world, and matter is the sole reality; movement is conceivable only if there be empty space into which bits of matter can swerve; everything we see must be explained as aggregates of atoms, uncreatable and indestructible (x–xi). Consequently, there is no room in the universe for anything such as the Roman religion Lucretius attacked, above all no room for piety, founded on a relationship between the gods and humanity when there is none. Against the pusillanimous debility of cringing piety, Lucretius opposes the Epicurean message that the gods are indifferent, that human existence ends with death, and that accepting the truth gives peace.

> Piety isn't to come in humble access,
> on view and vested, daily to stone and altar,
> to fall prostrate on earth and spread the hands
> in hallowed halls, to flood the temple floors

with animal blood, and string prayer into prayer,
but the power to view a world without dismay.
V. 1198–1203

While the problem Lucretius intends to overcome is the very existence of religion, Newman's specialty is the close examination of the difficulties the natural man
faces when confronted by mysterious religious truths which baffle the senses and
demand a total overhaul of attitudes and aims. *Parochial Sermons*'s last two volumes
present Christian life as fostered by the celebration of the liturgical seasons. The
crucial reality which is explored in the Advent sermons which open Volume 5 is
spiritual vision, which reverses the rationalist's reliance upon occular vision as the
test of truth, a presumption embedded in the adage that "seeing is believing." Just
the reverse holds true with the realities of Faith and the supernatural destiny
promised by Christ, for in those matters "believing is seeing." The epigraph shared
by all four members of the volume's Advent cluster is Isaiah's prophecy that "Thine
eyes shall see the King in His beauty: they shall behold the land that is very far off."
This prophecy will be fulfilled in Zion, where the great King will reward those who
have stood fast against oppression. Our natural eyes do not now see the King, but
they "shall" do so, and "shall behold" the land of promise. For Newman, living in
the bright day of Christ's Redemption rather than in the Old Law's time of shadows, that prophecy has already in part been fulfilled, since for the Christian
"believing is seeing."

Opening the Advent group, "Worship, A Preparation for Christ's Coming"
does not celebrate Jesus' historical birth in Bethlehem but instead meditates upon
our standing face-to-face with Christ at the moment of our death, that being the
"Coming" of Christ most critical for us individually. As Newman begins the sermon, the dampness and chill of the year's end represents the world's exhaustion,
because while life is "well enough in its way" it "does not satisfy," and therefore the
soul is content to be "cast forward upon the future." To the extent that its perception is "keen and true," it will in fact "rejoice solemnly that 'the night is far spent,
the day is at hand'" when we shall at last "see the King in His beauty." In harmony with the mood of the season, the Christian should reflect that "appearing
before God, and dwelling in His presence," is very different from being bound by
a system of moral laws. Standing before God requires "a special preparation of
thought and affection," one that will enable us "to endure his countenance." Such
a preparation is best provided by the "worship and service of God" in His Church.

Newman offers an analogy that clarifies the borderline condition in which we
enjoy a genuine sight of God, yet one that is not visible to the eye. The Israelites,
when Moses descended from Mount Sinai, found themselves too dazzled by the radiance emanating from his face to endure it without that glow being dampened by

a covering veil, which provides the analogy that Newman uses in order to clarify his point.

> That veil is so far removed in the Gospel, that we are in a state of preparation for its being altogether removed. We are with Moses in the Mount so far, that we have a sight of God; we are with the people beneath it so far, that Christ does not visibly show Himself. He has put a veil on, and He sits among us silently and secretly. When we approach Him, we know it only by faith; and when He manifests Himself to us, it is without our being able to realize to ourselves that manifestation. 5.8–9

Meeting Christ requires courage, which is "gained by steady thought." Courage being needed for the life of Faith, the best way to think steadily about Christ's coming to us at death is to celebrate the "sacramental Ordinances" of the Church. This advice applies most fully to "Holy Seasons, which include in them the celebration of many Ordinances." By this facilitating means, the Church calendar helps us to attain "chastened hearts and religious eyes."

Newman's exploration of spiritual vision is continued by "Reverence, A Belief in God's Presence," and again he uses a parallel with Moses to clarify his presentation. As Moses could not enter the promised land but was allowed to see it "from a distance," we too, not "admitted to heavenly glory," are allowed "to see much, in preparation for seeing more." Christ lives in His Church really though invisibly, and in its rites "fulfils" the promise of the epigraph from Isaiah, for the words of the Prophet "relate to our present state" as well as to the next world. However, most people cannot comprehend this truth because "they do not realize the presence of Christ," nor admit "the duty of realizing it." If they did, they would act more reverently.

Taken together, two classes of Christians deficient in reverence "go far to make up" the religious portion of the community. First, those who think the Church's creed "too strict" and suppose that "no certain doctrines" need to be believed, because the important thing is that one's conduct be "respectable and orderly." Second, those convinced that they were born children of wrath but who believe that God "so absolutely forgives" their habitual transgressions that they have "nothing to answer for." Both think the Almighty to be without exception a God of love, "the one meaning by love *benevolence*, the other *mercy*," but neither regard Him with respectful fear. The heart of the sermon is Newman's catalog of the signs showing their deficiency in reverence. They will, for example, describe their conversion and state of sanctification as if they knew their spiritual condition "as well as God knows it." Another sign is their careless manner of discussing Jesus' earthly life and action, "as if He were a mere man." Other sorts of conduct which indicate their lack of reverence include

the freedom with which [they] propose to alter God's ordinances to suit their own convenience, or to meet the age; their reliance on their private and antecedent notions about
sacred subjects; . . . their contempt for any view of the Sacraments which exceeds the evidence of their senses; and their confidence in settling the order of importance in which the
distinct articles of Christian faith stand;—-all which shows that it is no question of words
whether men have fear or not, but that there *is* something they really have not, whatever
name we give it. 5.21

One group supposes fear and awe "inconsistent with reason, the other with the
Gospel," and thus both neglect the duty of reverence on principle. To the contrary,
says Newman, there are emotions we would experience if we literally saw God, and
"if we realize His presence" we will feel them. The sermon's georgic advice is to
kneel during prayer, not gawk about in Church, come often to Communion and
the like.

Newman's investigation of spiritual vision, especially as it is thwarted, continues in "Unreal Words." Here, the criticism is softer than it was in the previous sermon, for talking-without-meaning is commonly a misfortune that stems from our
imperfect condition, rather than from any culpable infraction of correct relations
with God. To be sincere is "really to see with your minds" the wonderful things
Christ has done. In contrast to the Old Law, where God revealed Himself visibly
to Jacob, Moses, Isaiah and others, to us He reveals Himself "not visibly, but more
wonderfully and truly," in that He does so "not without the cooperation of our own
wills but upon our faith." Spiritual vision is not automatic and inevitable, like occular vision in those with unimpaired sight. It is not something that happens to us
but something that we do, something within our reach that must be reached for.
Thus St. Paul prays for the Ephesians "that Christ may dwell in their hearts by
faith," and that "the eyes of their understanding" might be enlightened.

Having clarified the nature of spiritual vision as an acquired capability,
Newman catalogues some of the ways in which, in ordinary life and in the life of
Faith, people "make unreal professions, or seeing see not, . . . and speak without
mastering, or trying to master, their words." As in "Reverence, A Belief . . .," the
heart of this sermon too is the articulation of disability. But here the focus is on the
psychological substratum, the reasons underlying the inattention, so to call it,
which causes people to run their vocabularies without accurately speaking their
minds. This conceptual lassitude Newman sees as not caused by the deliberate
intent to deceive self and others so much as by a reluctance to confess the real state
of their convictions and feelings. And commonly, the root cause is the problem we
all face in attempting to understand either ourselves or the truths of religion when
we have given careful attention to neither. As Newman explains, doctrines such
as original sin, Christ's divinity and atonement, or the crucial role of baptism are
too hard to grasp "without very complicated and profound feelings." If someone

"simply and genuinely believes the doctrines, he must have these feelings." But "absolute belief is the work of long time," and absenting the completion of that work, a man's "profession of feeling outruns the real inward existence of feeling, or he becomes unreal." Yes, we ought to "have our hearts penetrated with the love of Christ," but if they are not, "professing that they are does not make them so."

This common disparity between one's profession and the limited extent to which it is validated by genuine belief frequently occurs in the young, since those "who have never known sorrow or anxiety" lack the "depth and seriousness" which only longer experience can produce. Yet this is not a fault in them but simply "a plain fact." Much more does profession deviate from reality in persons who "have some secret motive urging them a different way from religion," which puts them "into an unnatural course," for which they are not wholly guiltless. Yet the behavior Newman has been instancing "is often a misfortune," because a long time is needed to "really feel and understand things as they are." Thus Newman concludes "Unreal Words" not with an indictment of error so much as with a description of the difficulty we all face in mastering a way of seeing that is acquired only through persistent effort over a long time.

> We ever promise things greater than we master, and we wait on God to enable us to perform them. Our promising involves a prayer for light and strength . . . we all say the Creed, but who comprehends it fully? All we can hope is, that we are in the way to understand it. 5.43

To examine Volume 5's Advent sermons is to recognize that once "Worship, A Preparation for Christ's Coming" has established a seasonal context, the remaining three sermons address different audiences and problems: first, irreverent Christians who think decent conduct all that matters or who think God automatically forgives their sins; second, those who commonly fall victim to unreal words from inexperience; and third, devout Christians whose anxieties are addressed in "Shrinking from Christ's Coming." This third group does not shrink because they fear death but because, should it occur immediately, the Lord's Coming would shorten the time they need to purify their motives and conduct. "Shrinking from" is a sermon about emotion, anxiety, hope and fear. In his Treatise on Human Acts, Aquinas says "the object of hope is a future good, difficult but possible to obtain," while in contrast "the object of fear is a future evil," one which appears hard to avoid. Most interestingly, it is love which causes fear, for it is through loving a certain good [such as being prepared for some critical event] that "whatever deprives a man of that good is an evil to him" (IaIIae 41:2, 43:2).

Because hope and fear produce anxiety even in the most ordinary of circumstances, much more will that be the case in boundary situations, such as facing any crucial, unknown future or experiencing events that explode one's conception of what normal reality allows. Newman begins the sermon by recollecting along with his audience the mixture of "fear and comfort" experienced by Mary Magdalen and the other Mary when in Matthew's Gospel they arrive at the sepulchre just in time to feel the shaking of the earthquake and see the angel roll back the stone from the door, sit down upon it and tell them that Jesus "is risen as he said" and that they are to "go quickly and tell his disciples." Anybody would react as they did. They "trembled and were amazed," departing from the tomb "'with fear and great joy.'" The Apostles, too, when suddenly Jesus stood among them, "were terrified and affrighted." The uniformity of human nature guarantees that when contemplating one's own meeting Christ at death, such reflection naturally causes trepidation. As Newman asks rhetorically, "Can any look forward to it with joy" when not assured of his own salvation? The difficulty becomes even greater when we "pray for its coming soon."

Newman examines the paradox that the Christian "should in all things be sorrowful yet rejoicing," an agenda which would be easier if our spiritual vision were "keen enough to follow out the lines of God's providence." He offers a number of points for overcoming the apparent contradiction, beginning with the thought that even if "our feelings about ourselves" cannot be reconciled to "the command given us," our duty is to obey the command. His second suggestion is that when we pray "that He would come," we pray also "that He may draw us while He draws near us," making us holier as he approaches. Third, "the more your soul becomes one with Him who deigns to dwell within it, the more it sees with His eyes." Christ asks "not sinlessness, but diligence," and therefore the effort itself counts for us. However, these points or considerations strike us as paper arguments rather than consolation directed to the anxious heart. Yet Newman's final argument does offer sympathetic support.

> But once more. You ask, how can you make up your mind to stand before your Lord and God; I ask in turn, how do you bring yourself to come before Him now day by day?——for what is this but meeting Him? Consider what it is you mean by praying, and you will see that, at the very time that you are asking for the coming of His kingdom you are anticipating that coming, and accomplishing the thing you fear. When you pray, you come into His presence. Now reflect on yourself, what your feelings are in coming. They are these: you seem to say,— -I am in myself nothing but a sinner . . . I know He is All-holy, yet I come before Him . . . Why do I do so? First of all, for this reason. To whom should I go? . . . I have an instinct within me which leads me to rise and go to my Father . . . This is the feeling in which we come to confess our sins, and to pray to God for pardon day by day; and observe, it is the very feeling in which we must prepare to meet Him when He comes visibly. 5.54–5

Finally, Newman transitions from communing with God in prayer, to receiving Christ in Holy Communion, which "is in very form an anticipation of His coming, a near presence of Him in earnest of it." Many people, feeling that to be the truth, neglect Holy Communion, and thus "deprive themselves of the highest blessing" Christians have in this world. Concluding the sermon, Newman reminds his audience that God is "mysteriously threefold," that while the Father remains in heaven, Christ comes to judge the world, and while He is so engaged, he is with us, "bearing us up and going forth to meet Himself." We do not go to meet Him alone, since He accompanies us.

In contrast to the anxious sense of anticipation which characterizes the volume's Advent reflections, the five Christmas sermons meditate upon the seasonally appropriate emotional tonality which emphasizes peacefulness, gratitude and contentment. Newman has arranged these sermons so that they form a triptych, the central panel being "The Mystery of Godliness," on the Incarnation. This panel is flanked by two pairs of sermons which lead into and follow from the pivotal theological reflection. The initial pair describes the distinctive qualities of the Christian character along with the feeling state most consonate with Christ's having recast human nature on our behalf. The other pair reflects on the theological history of humanity from Adam's creation to our new birth in Christ, which has restored us not to the original prelapsarian state but to a paradise of which Adam, and our own childhood, are both types. Further, this second pair provides a segue from the Christmas spirit of trustful peace to the Epiphany season's greater outreach to others, its initial sermons attacking important theological errors by correcting the misreadings of St. Paul's Epistles from which those errors spring.

Our redemption is not the result of remote negotiation with a far-off God but is instead a family affair, for, as the epigraph of "The Mystery of Godliness" states it, "both He that sanctifieth and they who are sanctified are all of one." He and we are close relations, brothers. Christ is our brother by virtue of the Incarnation, through which, "having sanctified our nature in Himself," He communicates that nature to us. This is the mystery of godliness, which should be present to our minds "especially at this season," when Christ took our flesh, "without spot of sin, to make us clean from all sin." To accomplish this, He took our nature into Himself "in a way above nature," by-passing human fatherhood in order to be conceived by the Holy Ghost of the Virgin Mary. This is the great mystery "of which mercy is the beginning and sanctity the end."

According to one of those georgic figures which thread through *Parochial Sermons*, Christ is the "engrafted Word, which is able to save our souls." Though it appears that Christ is engrafted into *us*, the direction of dependence is just the reverse, because we are the scions, the cuttings grafted into the Word of God, who thereafter depend on His life to raise us above the state of nature and provide us a share in the life of the Trinity. That is why Christmas

> is especially the season of grace. We come to see and experience God's mercies . . . This is
> a time for innocence, and purity, and gentleness, and mildness, and contentment, and peace

> . . . Christ comes at other times with garments dyed in blood; but now He comes to us in
> all serenity and peace, and He bids us rejoice in Him, and love one another. 5.97–8

The first pair of flanking sermons which accompany and highlight "The Mystery of Godliness," i.e., "Equanimity" and "Remembrance of Past Mercies," position the Incarnation in a temporal context that reaches back beyond the Apostles to the patriarchs of the Old Testament, who shared certain religious attitudes which are admirable and imitable. St. Paul's advice to ever "Rejoice in the Lord" is the keynote of "Equanimity," a sermon which presents "a distinct view of the Christian character" based upon "a calm and cheerful mind." What Newman finds most surprising is that Paul—who had a volatile temper, and suffered shipwreck, stoning and the care of the churches during a time when the Church was rocked by agitations and commotions—presents a picture of the Christian character so free of excitement and so full of repose as though *Philippians* had been written "in some monastery of the desert or some country parsonage." The Christian's distinctive traits are that he is dispassionate and "careful for nothing," because, knowing how things will end, "he cares less for the road which is to lead to it." His contentment is never shrill, arm-waving enthusiasm but a "deep, silent, hidden peace" which the world cannot see. The Christian at his most authentic is easy, kind, gentle and unassuming, without pretense or affectation, because "he has neither hope nor fear about this world." Newman is careful to distinguish the Christian's mental outlook from its worldly look-alike, one that, if "composed and candid," is built upon a wholly different foundation.

> In this day especially it is very easy for men to be benevolent, liberal, and dispassionate. It
> costs nothing to be benevolent when you feel nothing, to be cheerful when you have
> nothing to fear, to be generous or liberal when what you give is not your own, and to be
> benevolent and considerate when you have no principles and no opinions. Men nowadays
> are moderate and equitable, not because the Lord is at hand, but because they do not feel
> that He is coming. Quietness is a grace, not in itself, only when it is grafted on the stem of
> faith, zeal, self-abasement, and diligence. 5.71

Here once again we encounter the figure of grafting, which is applicable to Christians in many ways because Christ has come to raise the natural man beyond the natural condition, which is accomplished by the figural operation of grafting him into the divine life. Sometimes the grafting is God's operation alone, while at other times, as in this passage, it is an action ("grafted on the stem of grace") wherein God and man cooperate, the "grace" being God's contribution to the joint effort, the rest being up to the Christian who increases by his own diligence the talents given him.

"Remembrance of Past Mercies" continues the theme of thankfulness that culminates in "The Mystery of Godliness," or God's gift of His Son and our appreciative acceptance of it. Newman takes Jacob, David and St. Paul to be the three great exemplars of gratitude, because in them "a perishing wanderer had unexpectedly become a patriarch; a shepherd, a king; and a persecutor, an apostle." Each was chosen for a great purpose by God, and, while struggling to fulfil that purpose, continued to praise the Lord for making him His instrument. Of these three, Newman selects Jacob for close examination, prompted to that choice by the First Lesson for the Second Sunday after Christmas, a text taken from Isaiah ("Thou art my servant; I have chosen thee") "in which the Church is addressed and comforted under the name of Jacob," our standard-bearer in thankfulness.

To make his exposition more crisply effective, Newman provides us an extended contrast between Abraham and Jacob. Abraham followed God boldly and kept his affections "loose from everything earthly," being ready at the divine command to sacrifice his only son, while Jacob had many sons and "indulged them overmuch." Abraham impresses us as "looking forward in hope" and Jacob as "looking back in memory"; the one patriarch "making his way towards the promises," the other "musing over their fulfilment." If Abraham neither feared nor felt the world, Jacob recoiled and "winced, as being wounded by it." Jacob's characteristic strength was the retrospective capacity to remember (as Newman expresses it, "lovingly to trace") the wonderful things which God had done for him. It is this attitude of utter dependence on divine providence along with "thankfulness under it" which we ought to admire and imitate. For along with Jacob, we have these two duties, "to be resigned and to be thankful."

The second pair of flanking sermons do not continue the first pair's focus on thankfulness and joy but instead sharpen the contrast between the Christmas ideal and the imperfect reality. For although Christ's renewal of human nature is the unique and indispensable Divine Intervention celebrated during this season, from another perspective that renewal is a gradual Providential act which progresses over time like the leavening effect of yeast. The epigraph of "The State of Innocence" is the statement that although God "hath made man upright, they have sought out many inventions," and that waywardness continues in spite of the Incarnation. There *has* been progress, for our nature has gone through "much evil to greater good" and the flaming sword no longer bars the entrance to Eden, although we have yet to regain that paradisal state. The principle to which Newman draws attention is this, that while "the past *never* returns," God's providential intentions "move forward . . . like circles expanding about one center." That is why "in the past we see the future as if in miniature and outline."

Following the trajectory of his own insight, Newman describes briefly a five-phase typological progression in which Adam's primordial state of uprightness is reiterated, or echoed "like circles expanding about one center." Thus Eden's paradise can be recognized "in miniature or outline" in the Mosaic Law, which prefigures the Gospel, itself the anticipation of the garden-like state of rest after death, which points towards our future of eternal bliss in heaven. Now were the sermonist to attempt a full-dress articulation of this figural development, his exposition would certainly require far more ingenuity and persistence than an ordinary audience can stay alert enough to profit from. Therefore, he wisely truncates his design to a more modest comparison of Eden with childhood, saying that we "may well look back" on Eden as we would "on our own childhood" because it is "a type of the perfect Christian state," his authority being Jesus' insight that unless we become as little children we cannot enter the kingdom. Adam at his creation along with childhood sincerity and innocence are equally types of "our regenerate state in Christ," a state higher than either but figured by both. Developing the parallel to acknowledge equally human failure and the reality of Christian progress towards holiness, Newman says that

> this gift which sanctified Adam and saves children, does become the ruling principle of Christians generally when they advance to perfection. According as habits of holiness are matured, principle, reason, and self-discipline are unnecessary; a moral instinct takes their place in the breast, or rather, to speak more reverently, the Spirit is sovereign there. There is no calculation, no struggle, no self-regard, no investigation of motives. We act from love. 5.109

Unfortunately, great numbers of people "think that it is slavish and despicable to go on in that narrow way in which they are brought up as children." Here is the point which pivots the sermon into the second phase of its two-part structure, which investigates the contrastive element of defection from Providential intention. The remainder of the sermon addresses the contest of Faith and Intellect, the latter being the root cause of the "many inventions" lamented by *Ecclesiastes*. Happily, the natural desire for God, even when abused and denied, is never quite strangled in its cradle. Ever since the Fall "the secret stirrings of God's grace" have prompted individuals to seek Him out, though they have done so "in a grovelling sort, like worms working their way upwards through the dust of the earth, turning evil against itself." Because worms do well enough working through the earth but are not known for attacking one another, Newman quickly modifies the figure so that the worms are displaced by ravenous serpents:

> Such too seems to be one chief way in which Providence carries on His truth . . . not by a direct flood of light upon the Church, but by setting one mischief upon another, bidding one serpent destroy another, the less the greater; thus gradually thinning the brood of sin . . . And in this way doubtless we are to regard sects and heresies, as witnesses and confessors of particular truths, as God's means of destroying evil. 5.111–12

The insight that heresy serves truth by cancelling out contrary errors gives way to Newman's concluding remarks on intellect itself "as exercised in the world."

VISIONARY SEASONS | 95

Intelligence is "a fruit of the fall," a power which "at the utmost" is merely "toler-
ated in the Church" on account of its tendency to run amok. Reflecting on the civilized advances of his century, Newman asks "what is all its intellectual energy but
a fruit of the tree?" What place have its "splendours, triumphs, speculations, or theories in the pure and happy region which was our cradle, or in that heaven which
is to be our rest?"

Concluding the Christmas sermons, "Christian Sympathy" reflects upon the
common nature, feelings, aspirations and destiny of all members of the Church. By
raising our human nature, Christ overcame the effects of the Fall, which was pre-
cipitated by Adam's desire to become "as gods" through god-like knowledge of good
and evil. Paradoxically, Christ became man so that men "through brotherhood with
Him, might in the end become as gods." Wherever found and in whatever state of
soul, the Christian is one and the same. As in Christ, "who is perfect," so in himself, "who is training towards perfection." Translating this to the interpretive
vocabulary of Pauline theology, "as in righteousness which is *imputed* to him in fulness, so in that righteousness which is *imparted* to him only in measure, and not yet
in fulness" (my italics). Since they have the same nature, aspirations and difficulties in common, Christians ought to sympathize with one another, sharing their
hopes and fears more candidly. Unfortunately, says Newman, they are cowed by "the
opinions of the age," which have their strength "in their public recognition." As
a result Christians commonly "dare not even realize to themselves" their own
religious judgments, much less share their thoughts with others.

> Thus it is that the world cuts off the intercourse between soul and soul, and substitutes idols
> of its own for the one true Image of Christ, in and through which only souls can sympathize.
> Their best thoughts are stifled . . . Such is the power of false creeds to fetter the mind and
> bring it into captivity; false views of things, of facts, of doctrines, are imposed on it . . . ,
> and men live and die in bondage, who were destined to rise to the stature of the fulness of
> Christ. 5.124

Here, Newman introjects the transitional observation which brings the volume to
the theological preoccupation of the Epiphany sermons, more particularly the
first four of them, i.e., the careful examination of the "false creeds" which have
arisen through theological misperceptions of St. Paul's epistles.

> Such [false creeds], for example, I consider to be, among many instances, the interpretation
> which is popularly received among us at present, of the doctrinal portion of St. Paul's
> Epistles, an interpretation which has troubled large portions of the Church for a long three
> hundred years. 5.124–5

After this segue to the Epiphany cluster, Newman concludes "Christian
Sympathy" with the reflection that the standard of holiness in England may be so
low because Christians are afraid to embrace the correct understanding of Scriptural

truth, mistaking that "as a cause of estrangement" from others "which really would be a bond of union" with them.

The third liturgical season celebrated in Volume 5, Epiphany, usually emphasizes this three-fold manifestation of Christ to the world: the Magi coming to adore the Child Saviour in Bethlehem, the baptism which revealed Jesus as the Son of God, and the miracle of the wine at Cana which showed his power over the physical world. However, Newman turns from these traditional themes to focus upon St. Paul, the Apostle to the Gentiles, who clarified the significance of the Saviour's coming and whose conversion is celebrated during late January, within Epiphany's temporal ambit. The initial four of Newman's eight Epiphany sermons bring the theological portions of St. Paul's Epistles up to date for his own time—not by discovering new meanings in them but by restoring orthodox interpretation which was corrupted in "large portions of the Church" during three hundred years. The second group of four sermons reflects on the practical significance St. Paul's hortatory insights.

The title of the first Epiphany sermon, "Righteousness Not of Us, but in Us," contains in small compass Newman's entire argument, as his titles so frequently do. Its two critical prepositions seesaw across the hinge of the medial comma, the "of Us" presumption of the Corinthians, as St. Paul sees them, balancing against the "in Us" correction that Newman makes of a rather different error. Reflecting upon *I Corinthians*, he recognizes that St. Paul's original audience "seem to have thought" that their spiritual gifts were their own "by a sort of right," because they could boast "more cultivation of mind than others." But in truth their power to pray, their baptism, and their growth in holiness were all from Christ, the "foundation" of their righteousness, while a humble and self-abased heart is "the ground and soil in which the foundation must be laid." That is, two parties are involved in human salvation, and it is critically important to achieve the correct balance between God's doing and man's. Neglecting to do that makes the Christian vulnerable to a pair of dangerous errors.

> On the one hand, it is but building on sand to profess to believe in Christ, yet not to acknowledge that without Him we can do nothing. It is what is called the Pelagian heresy, of which many of us perhaps have heard the name. [. . . and] as there are those who consider that life, righteousness, and salvation are of us, so there are others who hold that they are not in us [when in fact] justification must be in a man if it is to profit him. And it is hard to say which of the two errors is the greater. 5.134–7

Christians in this world are always a work in progress. If sanctification were "finished as regards individuals," then why did the Holy Spirit come? The Spirit came to complete in us what Christ had already completed "in Himself, but left unfinished as regards us." In opposite ways, both those persons who think that salvation "is not of God" and those who suppose that it "is not in ourselves" equally deprive the Christian life of "its mysteriousness."

"The Law of the Spirit" expands upon the theme sounded late in the first sermon, i.e., the work of the Holy Ghost. Newman's symbol of this error is the Jews whose allegiance to the Mosaic Law prompted their rejection of the Gospel. He sees the Law of Moses as "the nearest approximation of" the Law of God which was available "in its place and age," and concurs with the Prophets that Adam's fall generated an unrighteous state, that is, "knowing the Law, but not doing it; admiring, not loving; assenting, not following it." If that condition is now revoked for Christians, by what means was the revocation brought about? By the gift of Christ's Passion enhanced through "the abiding influence of the Holy Ghost" which allows us to offer God "acceptable obedience." If the Law of the Spirit has surpassed the Mosaic Law, what is the correct understanding of how unrighteous persons can become righteous in God's eyes? For one thing, the work of the Spirit, "though imperfect, considered as ours, is perfect as far as it comes from Him." The result is that our own works, when "done in the Spirit of Christ, have a justifying *principle* in them," i.e., the Spirit's Presence. The other reason why we are dealt with as being righteous is "for what is ours;——not indeed what is now ours, but for what" through God's mercy "we shall be." The problem which the unbelieving Jews could not work around was pride, which kept them from coming "suppliantly for the gift of the Spirit," since they considered faith to be "something mean and weak." Moreover, they considered themselves God's chosen people "by a sort of right," such that they did not need grace, being confident that "their outward ceremonies and their dead works would profit them." The expression "dead works" is the segue into the next Epiphany sermon.

"The New Works of the Gospel" answers the objection brought by some people, that if the New Covenant "be of works too, how is the Gospel other than the Law?" Through this way of thinking, some persons conclude that "salvation under the Gospel is *not* of works," but entirely of faith. Approaching this objection historically, Newman points out that although salvation under the Gospel truly is new, "in certain respects" religion still is what the Jews, and the heathen along with them, had long thought it to be. "The way of justification has in all religions been by means of works; so it is under the Gospel; but in the Gospel alone it is by means of good works." Putting off temporarily any account of good works, Newman summarizes some of the many parallels in "doctrine and worship" in all known religions, parallels which are not surprising because "the worship of God" cannot escape having a certain commonality everywhere. All religions include the saying of prayers, postures of devotion, meetings for communal worship, a large organized body with orders and officers, ministers and people, with a powerful influence over the state. All religions have had their mysteries, i.e., their "alleged disclosures of Truth, which could not be fully understood all at once, if at all, and which were open to some more than to others." And all religions have observed holy days, celebrated festivals, used water for purification, and built religious temples. Having summarized these commonalities, Newman comes to his theological point: when St. Paul says that "old things are passed away," when he says that "all things are new," he does not mean that those religious forms which flourished before Christ's coming suddenly became obsolete, worthless. By *"new,"* St. Paul means that "they are *renewed."* By "old things *passing away* he signifies that they are *changed."* Religion still has "forms, ordinances, precepts, mysteries, duties, assemblies, festivals, and temples as of old time." But whereas these had before been carnal and dead, "since Christ came, they have a life in them." Thus the objection Newman had stated at the sermon's outset has been answered, though the right understanding of good works has yet to be explained, a task performed by the fourth of the Epiphany sermons which undertake to correct misreadings of St. Paul.

"The State of Salvation" explains that God does not at death change the state of Christians. He "brings them into a saving state here, preparatory to heaven," and this state "all must enter here who shall be saved hereafter." Not all Christians accept this truth. Some do not believe that human nature can be genuinely holy "even when regenerate." Others suppose "a man may be an habitual sinner, and yet be in a state of salvation, and in the kingdom of heaven." Both are in error, especially the latter, because as Newman puts it, "a state of salvation is so far from being a state in which sins of every kind are forgiven, that it is a state in which there are not sins of every kind to forgive." The evidence he offers to oppose such errors and clarify the use of good works is found in Jesus' parables, which reveal that authentic Christians lessen the distance between themselves and God by performing good works. The parables of the Ten Virgins, the Talents, and the Wedding Guest show us that the state of a true Christian, "as our Lord contemplates it, is one in which he is not lamenting the victories of sin, but working out salvation" through a steady, sincere and effective "course of obedience." This sermon having stated the principle, the next two transition from correction of errors into moral reflections upon human conduct in light of St. Paul's theology.

"Transgressions and Infirmities" distinguishes between serious violations of divine law and imperfections of which no one is wholly free: "Faith keeps us from transgressions, and they who transgress, for that very reason have not true faith." As Newman defines them, transgressions include all vicious habits, covetousness, violent breaches of charity, profaneness, heresy, and false worship, along with hardness of heart. It does transgressors no good that, as Scripture says, faith is imputed "for righteousness," for their faith is illusory; "instead of faith blotting out transgressions, transgressions blot out faith." This is "a holy doctrine" because it "provides for our pardon without dispensing with obedience."

The follow-on sermon, "Sins of Infirmity," explores a percipient observation, i.e., that "we arrive at holiness through infirmity." This is not the paradox it might seem, for "man's very condition is a fallen one, and in passing out of the country of sin," he cannot help but pass through it. Infirmities are sins which "stain us, though without such consent of the will as to forfeit grace." Thus, for instance, original sin is a mystery, baptism so removes it that the guilt is forgiven us, "but still the infection of it remains." Involuntary sins can arise from former habits of sin, even those which are "long abandoned." Infirmities often arise from the lack of self-command, "the mind being possessed of more light than strength, the conscience being informed, but the governing principle weak." These sins include excessive feelings of grief, of anger, impatience, fear, and so on. Other examples would include difficulty rising from bed, eating and drinking just what one should, inability to fix one's mind on prayer, or to regulate one's thought to exclude things that should be kept out. Lastly, transgressions caused by lack of practical experience would fall into the category of infirmities. These, says Newman in closing, are some of the classes of sins which can be found "where the will is right, and faith lively." These infirmities are "not inconsistent with the state of grace."

The last two Epiphany sermons move from sins to mental states, which can either be ordered towards self-deception or, to the contrary, can accurately testify to our upright conduct. The first, "Sincerity and Hypocrisy," begins with the starkest contrast between open sinners and consistent Christians. It presents this utter dissimilarity to open a space "between the two," a space occupied by the hypocrite, who acts with the one while speaking like the other. While the genuine Christian has "an honest, unaffected *desire* of doing right" in God's eyes, the double-minded or "nominal" Christian has "other ends besides the truth." As a result, one finds in such persons

> an inconsistency in conduct, and a half-consciousness (to say the least) of inconsistency, and a feeling of the necessity of defending oneself to oneself, and to God, and to the world; in a word, hypocrisy; these are the signs of the merely professed Christian. 5.224

Given the nominal Christian's presupposition that there are two opponents involved in the religious life, God and self, one is not surprised to find "that reasoning and argument is the mode in which he approaches his Saviour and Judge." Such was the conduct of the Pharisees in Jesus' time also. When they challenged Him by inquiring what authority He had for teaching and performing miracles, Christ replied with his own duplicity-unmasking question about John's baptism. On the one hand, they preferred to "deny John" rather than to acknowledge Him. Yet on the other hand, "they dare not openly deny the Baptist, because of the people; so, between hatred of our Lord and dread of the people, they would give no answer at all. 'They reasoned among themselves,' we are told." Newman finds an equivalent tendency in the nominal Christian.

The Epiphany group is concluded by "The Testimony of Conscience," which states that we can be innocent and have a "sense of" our innocence such that "the thought of God's eye being upon us" makes us happy. The half-hearted cannot feel this contentment. Such was the young ruler that "came running" to present himself before Christ, Who straightaway "exposed what was in his heart" and left him to steal away quietly, sorrowing as he went. St. Peter, too, was half-hearted before Pentecost. His fault was not self-deception but "reserved devotion," for, in "one corner of his heart," his commitment was incomplete. Men in that condition, half doubting their own honesty, "make loud professions of it." Peter's protestation of commitment to Christ redoubled his grief when, following the resurrection, the Lord repeatedly inquired whether he loved Him. How different is this from being "really perfect in heart," having a "secret sense" of our own sincerity, though an assurance that does not "rise above a sober trust" that we are right with God.

While Epiphany can be treated as a liturgical season, though it lacks seasonal importance as compared with Advent and Easter, the three Sundays before Lent begins are not a "season" at all. The very names, Septuagesima, Sexagesima and Quinquagesima, indicate their derivative, place-holding purpose, as if they said "Lent and Easter are coming soon." But Newman in Volume 5 presents them as a makeshift pre-Lenten season, one he expands to seven sermons in order to raise the number of sermons in the volume to 24. One can see the practical use of expanding the three Sundays before Lent into a 7-sermon pre-Lenten "season," whose function is to prepare the audience for Lent either by recalling life's pleasant side before the onset of penitential self-denial, or by strengthening the will for the rigors soon to come. In their themes, the pre-Lenten sermons are of two kinds. One stresses resoluteness, which must be summoned up and enacted. The other emphasizes consolation, which is not an action but a placidness that must be received and accepted. The courage of resoluteness alternates in contrast with the unbought grace of consolation, though Newman is careful to avoid an annoying, sing-songy back-and-forth alternation in sermon positioning. Using "R" and "C" to identify the two thematic types, the sermons are presented in this sequence: R, C, R, R, C, C, R. These sermons will be discussed not seriatim, but as two thematically complementary sub-groups, beginning with the consolatory sub-set.

"Present Blessings" reminds us of the many things that make our lives pleasant and satisfying, such as the gift of natural life, family affection, even a good night's sleep. The believer enjoys such comforts along with everyone else, but he also enjoys distinctive blessings such as Christian brotherhood, the present peace of the Church, daily worship and weekly Holy Communion. Advocating a positive attitude, Newman reminds readers that gloom "is no Christian temper" and that the pain of self-chastisement must be "sweetened by faith and cheerfulness." After all, Jesus compares us to the birds of the air and the lilies of the field. Thus one need not search far to find reasons for being thankful, especially as Lent approaches.

> These thoughts are suitable on this day (Septuagesima Sunday), when we first catch a sight . . . of the Forty Days of Lent, [during which] we must rejoice while we afflict ourselves . . . Let us, then, on this day, dwell upon a thought which it will be a duty to carry with us through Lent, the thought of the blessings and mercies of which our present life is made up. 5.271

"The Thought of God, the Stay of the Soul" probes more deeply into human nature than does "Present Blessings," for it recognizes that until God is manifested in it, the soul "has faculties and affections without a ruling principle, object, or purpose." Says Newman,

> the happiness of the soul consists in the exercise of the affections, [. . . such that] when they are undeveloped, restrained, or thwarted, they are not happy. This is our real and true bliss. 5.314

That explains why the thought of God is "the happiness of man," which is the case whether the person is in a state of grace, or is trying to escape the state of sin. For the peace of a good conscience is the "habitual consciousness" that our hearts are not at enmity with God, along with the accompanying intention that we shall continue to be watched by the divine eye. Similarly, those who are gripped by the wish to repent their sins grow eager to afflict themselves. They do so out of love and gratitude to God, "horror of the past," of which they are now ashamed, and hunger to escape from their present condition and find their way to a "more heavenly" state.

The third consolation sermon of the sub-group, "Love, the One Thing Needful," explores the disconcerting fact that it is possible to obey God not out of love but rather "from a sort of conscientiousness," which is not affection but rather a motive arising "more from the fear of God than from love of Him." The evidence is not hard to find. For example, some people develop a habit of prayer in which they continue their devotions simply because of their own "regularity in observing them." Whenever a change in their circumstances derails the habit pattern, they stop praying. Another kind of evidence of love's absence in the conduct of Christians is their proneness to becoming engrossed with trifles, such as complaining about the lack of variety in their religious life, finding it distasteful to condescend "to men of low estate" and demanding "powerful preaching, or interesting and touching books, in order to keep our thoughts and feelings on God." Faults such as these Newman traces to "the comforts of life"—.a point which transitions toward the fast-approaching Lenten season, since, "at least at seasons," it is wise to "defraud ourselves of nature, if we would not be defrauded of grace."

The first of the pre-Lenten season's resoluteness sermons, "Many Called, Few Chosen," opposes the presumption that because God is good most people will get into heaven. Newman argues just the reverse by calling attention to the many emphatic Scriptural texts which proclaim the opposite, not only Jesus' "narrow is the way . . . and few there be that find it," and St. Paul's reflection that "as former-ly, 'there is a *remnant*'" only who will be saved, but Jeremiah and Ezekiel, too, "all teach the same doctrine," i.e., that in most cases God's "bountifulness" is answered by man's "ingratitude." Some think it is God's Will that only a few be saved, oth-ers protest that the narrow-way doctrine tends to make people "self-confident and uncharitable" to others. However, Newman argues to the contrary that it is just as "inexplicable" why God would act differently to different individuals as "why this man or that should act differently towards God." Secondly, he argues that it is not knowledge that the chosen are few which causes these bad feelings, "but a man's private assurance that *he* is chosen." In fact the doctrine that many are called but few chosen has no tendency to make individuals think "themselves secure and oth-ers reprobate," for this simple reason, that "we do not know the *standard* by which God will judge us." That being the state of the case, it is our practical wisdom not to speculate about things wherein we are so utterly ignorant. Given the complex-ity of the evidence upon which we will be either saved or damned, it is folly "to argue from what we see to what God knows, or from discerning whether the divine seed has taken root in particular minds."

"Endurance, the Christian's Portion," which adopts as its epigraph Jacob's lamentation upon the apparent loss of his sons that "all these things are against me," argues that what Jacob said dejectedly the Christian must accept, "not in dejection, not sorrowfully, or passionately, or in complaint," but with measured calmness, "as if confessing a doctrine." Newman's contemporaries commonly presumed that Scriptural passages such as Jacob's lamentation had become irrelevant, since in their view the Church is now at peace, "rights are secured to it, and privileges added," such that there is no danger to a Christian "putting himself in the front of the Christian fight, when that fight is a benefice or a dignity." That is what is said, both about the Church and about individuals. Newman has a different perspective, observing relevantly that Scripture cautions us to walk by faith, not by sight. The truth is that

> there is an inward world, which none see but those who belong to it; and though the out-side robe be many-coloured, like Joseph's coat, inside it is lined with camel's hair, or sack-cloth, fitting those who desire to be one with Him who fared hardly in the wilderness . . .
> There is an inward world into which they enter who come near to Christ, though to men in general they seem the same as before. 5.295

Newman's point is that, religion being so largely an unseen inward condition of soul, one should not be misled by the opinion that times are changed so that former difficulties have disappeared. To the contrary, the Church continues to fight the good fight, since while the Church "maintains her ground, she ever suffers in order to maintain it," and suffers "in proportion as she plays her part well." The Church's doctrines and practices "never can be palatable to the world"; if the world does not persecute, it can only be "because she does not preach."

"Affliction, A School of Comfort" focuses on St. Paul, and in particular the admirable example he set of learning by means of personal suffering how to sympathize with and comfort others who suffer. Newman in this sermon says

> At this season we commemorate [St. Paul's] conversion [a feast celebrated in late January]; and at this season we give attention, more than ordinary, to his Epistles. And on Sexagesima Sunday we almost keep another Festival in his memory, the Epistle for the day being expressly on the subject of his trials . . . [he having been beaten, chased about, imprisoned, shipwrecked, and stoned] that he might understand how poor a thing mortal life is, and might learn to contemplate and describe fitly the glories of the life immortal. 5.302

Having documented the appropriateness of meditating on St. Paul's conversion as Lenten self-denial comes nearer, Newman reminds us that suffering by itself has no power to make us holier. To the contrary, it makes many persons "morose, selfish, and envious." Austerity teaches some "to be cruel to others, not tender." Only in God's hand can affliction enable spiritual purification. Only "when grace is in the heart" could any earthly experience advance our salvation. The reason God brings His Saints into suffering is "that they may be what Christ was," that they might be led "to think of Him, not of themselves."

Finally, "The Power of the Will" [1 March, 1840] seems to have been written not only for Quinquagesima Sunday, but to conclude Volume 5 on the verge of Lent. Newman in this sermon distinguishes two kinds of Christians, those who use the grace extended them, and those, like the "unprofitable servant," who are "idle and worthless" by failing to bestir themselves. Such persons have not lost divine grace, yet they never realize that to achieve heaven it is "not enough to avoid evil." One must exert oneself and use the talents God has provided. Says Newman,

> As seeds have life in them, which seem lifeless, so the Body of Christ had life in itself, when it was dead; and so also . . . we too . . . have a spiritual principle in us, if we did but exert it . . . all the powers in the visible world are nothing to this gift within us . . . [why then do we] do so little, and instead of mounting with wings like eagles, grovel in the dust? . . . What is it we lack? The power? No; the will. 5.345

With this rousing call to spiritual exertion, Newman ends the first portion of his two-volume examination of the seasons of the liturgical year.

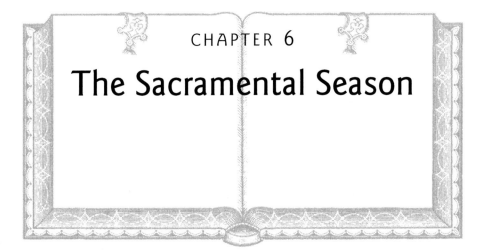

CHAPTER 6
The Sacramental Season

Newman calls the period from Ash Wednesday to Trinity Sunday "the Sacramental Season," a time in which Christians are especially "called to faith," the greatest of faith's mysteries being Christ's real presence in Holy Communion. Volume 6 reflects upon that portion of the liturgical year, beginning with a seven-member cluster of Lenten sermons. While Newman's entire collection consists of clusters of sermons which are interrelated and organized thematically, the first sermon group of Volume 6 adds something not seen before, a well orchestrated chronological presentation of its central theme. Because Christ's sacrificial death is a mystery, to rely upon argument would be futile, the more so when the preacher needs to motivate people to open their hearts to the mysterious reality that Lent celebrates.

To reach that goal, Newman arranges the six Sundays of Lent in a strategic progression aimed at arousing emotional attention and provoking the thoughts that are appropriately raised during the season. Instead of assigning one sermon for each week during Lent, he intentionally unbalances the sequence by limiting the first four weeks to three sermons (by subtitling them "First Sunday of Lent," "Second Sunday of Lent," and "Lent"), and then assigning four sermons to the two remaining weeks (two "Fifth Sunday of," two others "Sixth Sunday") of Lent. This sequential imbalance raises the emphasis upon the Passion by affectively anticipating Holy Week during the four Sundays before it begins. Using musical terms,

Newman creates a sermonic crescendo wherein the penitential stress of the earlier sermons gives way to the Christian's call to share in Christ's suffering through commemorative meditation.

The first three sermons of the Lenten cluster meditate on patterns of exemplary action, whether these be admirable or the reverse. In "Fasting a Source of Trial" Christ is the exemplary actor and the key term is "trial," because as Jesus fasted forty days in the desert and then was tempted by Satan, so too during Lent we are called upon to imitate Him. We are called, says Newman, "to become in a wonderful way" His members, the "visible form, or sacramental sign" of the Son of God, continuing the acts of His earthly life, in fasting, yes, but also in being tempted and triumphing over God's adversary. Newman seldom refers to Satan in *Parochial Sermons*, and then only briefly and in passing, but in "Fasting a Source of Trial" one finds the prince of darkness referred to more than a dozen times. Sometimes he is singular ("Satan" (6), "the devil" (2), "the evil one," "the adversary," "the accuser"), sometimes plural ("evil spirits," "the powers of hell"), but in every instance Newman's point is that "the truest view" of exercises like fasting is that "they open the next world for good and evil upon us." They make possible "an extraordinary conflict with the powers of evil." This vulnerability to conflict is "*an approach to God . . . yes, and to the powers of hell.*" But if we persevere, "we triumph with Christ." The intermediate position between earth and hell is that of the demoniac in the Gospel possessed by the dumb spirit whom the disciples could not cast out; in Mark's Gospel, after Jesus descends from the Transfiguration, He exorcizes that devil, explaining to his followers that "This kind can come forth by nothing but by prayer and fasting" (9: 29). Let us during Lent "look upon ourselves as on the Mount with Him," says Newman, gaining through spiritual exercises the strength we need to overcome Satan's wiles.

"Lent the Season of Repentance," the second member of the cluster, once again presents a reflection on exemplary action in the contrast between Esau and the Prodigal Son. The *Genesis* narrative of Esau, whom "at first sight we are disposed to pity," describes a person who is "profane" in selling his birthright, "and then presumptuous" in claiming the very birthright he had forfeited. As Newman uses him, Esau represents those Christians who, having sinned in the past, forget that they have done so and consequently do not "lament and deplore" their sins. As Adam and Eve parted too easily with their righteous condition for a mouthful of fruit, and as Esau surrendered his birthright "for a mess of lentils," so men nowadays lose theirs not for memorably wicked conduct but "commonly for the indulgence of general carelessness and spiritual sloth, because they do not like a strict life." Having done so, once again like Esau, they presume "that they stand just where they did, before they followed the world, the flesh, and the devil." The georgic good advice Newman offers them is to use the time of Lent to bewail and repent of their folly, thereby following the better example of the Prodigal Son, who did not presume to imagine that he still stood where he once had, but simply threw himself upon his father's mercy. "These are thoughts especially suited to this season" because the weeks before Easter "have been set apart every year, for the particular remembrance and confession of our sins."

"Apostolic Abstinence a Pattern for Christians" offers its audience a third template of exemplary action. From the epigraph, Paul's advice to Timothy "use a little wine for thy stomach's sake," one can infer that Timothy "was a man of mortified habits," which provides us the revelation that Apostolic Christians practiced abstinence from habit. As Newman says, the "great duty" of the Gospel is love to God and man, and the reason one should practice abstinence is that such love is "quenched by self-indulgence" while it is "cherished" by self-denial. Persons who enjoy this life too freely "make it or self their idol." Yet self-denial is worthless unless its motivation is love of God, since it is easy to be "amiable and upright" from a worldly motive. Acting from such an inferior intention cannot be corrected "by any one remedy," but abstinence and fasting help. Put another way, "You may think to dispense with fasting; true; and you may neglect to cultivate love."

These observations prepare us to recognize personal affection as the essence of our participation in Christ's redemptive passion, which later sermons in the Lenten group advocate. Foreseeing the objection that it is presumptuous for us to imitate the Apostles "that we may inherit the gifts of the spirit" as they did, Newman confesses that the charge is valid "so far as this," that presumptuousness can be charged if we "attempt *at once*" what they achieved. Yet God offers "second and third gifts" to those who improve His first, and "how high may be the spiritual faculties" He gives to those who cooperate with Him is beyond our power to know. The sermon concludes with the advice to begin "not with the end" but at the beginning, and to "mount up" a single step at a time, until it becomes "more painful" to indulge ourselves than to abstain, an experience "every one of common self-control must know."

These early sermons having dwelt upon the penitential facet of the season, "Christ's Privations a Meditation for Christians" transitions to the well-orchestrated crescendo leading towards the sacrificial death which is the season's apex. "As Easter draws nearer," the sermon begins, we are to confess our sins, but "especially" mourn the sufferings Christ endured "on account of them." That being the purpose of Lent, Newman poses rhetorical questions which focus attention on the common incapacity to rise to the call, as in asking, why have we "so little feeling" for His sacrifice that we "let the season come and go" without being moved? The reason why Christians are so often unresponsive, he suggests, is that they meditate so little. The cure is to recall what the Gospels say about Christ, and what is said about Him in Church, and do that "in a simple-minded, sincere, and reverential spirit," because such action is meditation. It is something that "even the most unlearned person" can manage, if he has the will.

The operational definition of meditation having been given, Newman provides his readers a timely caution, followed by a helpful observation. The caution is this, that meditation is at first "not at all pleasant" but "very irksome," since the mind will "gladly slip away" to focus on other matters. The helpful observation is that "by slow degrees" those who persist will discover that meditation softens their hearts, until "the history of Christ's trials and sorrows really moves us." By going on with it "quietly and steadily," it will eventually generate warmth, light and love, but their coming will be as silently unobtrusive as "the unfolding of the leaves in spring."

That ends the preparational introduction phase of the sermon, after which Newman provides his readers a sample meditation "by way of specimen," suggesting thoughts which can prepare Christians for seeing Christ in heaven and "for seeing Him in His Easter Festival." To summarize the heads of this specimen meditation, Christ came in poverty, being born in a stable to a poor woman; He endured cold and heat, slept in caves of the rock during His desert fasting, was often upon the sea at night, and was constantly journeying about the region. He was "a man of sorrows and acquainted with grief" even before He encountered the contempt, hatred and persecution of His Passion. Newman stops short of Holy Week ("I shall say little of it now, when His 'time is not come'"), though he does encroach to the extent of recalling the "overwhelming fear" which levelled Jesus in the Garden, as well as the "bitter stroke" of being betrayed to death by a close friend. Such is the "Meditation for Christians" promised by the sermon's title, after which Newman looks to the near approach of Holy Week and again extends a promise that sustained meditation will produce devotional results. "Deep feeling is but the natural or necessary attendant on a holy heart," which can be cultivated. Through meditation we can "gradually . . . be brought to these deep feelings."

Newman begins "Christ the Son of God Made Man," the second of the "Fifth Sunday in Lent" sermons of the Lenten cluster, with the chronological indicator "from this day, which is fourteen days before Easter, a more sacred season begins," one which has "more immediate reference" to Christ and is "especially consecrated" to thoughts of His Passion. In keeping with this change of emphasis, Newman reminds his audience of who and what Christ is, promising to speak "as simply and plainly" as do the Creeds. However, he devotes a considerable amount of space to correcting the widespread misapprehension of who and what Christ is—as we have seen him do repeatedly in *Parochial Sermons*. Newman makes four points in the sermon. First, Christ is God, from Eternity. Second, He is God *because* He is the Son of God, which leads the sermonist into his error-correction commentary.

And this is what makes the doctrine of our Lord's Eternal Sonship of such supreme importance, viz. that He is God because He is begotten of God; and they who give up the latter truth, are in the way to give up, or will be found already to have given up the former. The great safeguard of the doctrine of our Lord's Divinity is the doctrine of His Sonship; we realize that He is God only when we acknowledge Him to be by nature and from eternity Son. Nay, our Lord's Sonship is not only the guarantee to us of His Godhead, but also the condition of His incarnation. As the Son was God, so on the other hand was the Son suitably made man; it belonged to Him to have the Father's perfections, it became Him to assume a servant's form. 6.57–8

Drawing out the implications of what he has presented, Newman illustrates the manner in which people are liable to ignore the Church's Creeds and settle instead for their own natural understanding. The most serious of the theological errors are viewing Christ "as two separate beings, not as one Person; or again, of gradually forgetting or explaining away the doctrine of His Divinity altogether." To the contrary, key passages in St. John's Gospel "would seem to speak neither of Christ's human nature simply, nor of His divine, but of both together," for "where He was, there was the Father, and whoso had seen Him had seen the Father, whether we think of Him as God or as man." Newman's third point, Christ's mercy in taking upon Him our nature, and his fourth, Christ's acting through our nature without ceasing to be "what He was before," appear truncated after his expanded discussion of the second point, though in fact they can be as brief as they are because they ride upon the coattails of that commentary. After quoting the Athanasian Creed to endorse what he has just stated in his own words, Newman ends the sermon by observing that the Lenten season, when we are called to separate from the world and entertain "a subdued tone of thought and feeling," is an appropriate time to speak of the high mysteries of the faith. They are then "especially a comfort to us; but those who neglect fasting, make light of orthodoxy too." Clearly, Newman is unwilling to permit penitence to be forgotten as the sermon cluster moves towards the climax of Holy Week.

"The Incarnate Son, a Sufferer and Sacrifice," which is the first of the two sermons for "Sixth Sunday in Lent," begins with the time signpost that "we are now approaching that most sacred day when we commemorate Christ's passion and death," Newman's intention being not to provoke emotion but to offer "some serious thoughts" for the week. In this sermon, the temporal situation modulates from a crescendo rising towards the great events of Holy Week, to a timeless present, for "the Eternal Priest and His one ever-enduring Sacrifice," an action which was "completed once for all on Calvary," transcends time; it has now become a sempiternal event, one which "ever abideth," because it continues "ever present among us." When we commemorate Christ's passion, we activate in ourselves that supratemporal reality which will never surrender its effective presence in all times. As for the conduct of the sermon, Newman reiterates the conventionally recited events which constitute the passion, and does so because "what is plain is sometimes taken for granted by those who know it, and hence is never heard by others at all." Newman's presentation helps us to see that Christ's passion may be understood either as a sequential narrative of what happened in Jerusalem during that year's Passover celebration, or as what Christ enacted through His sufferings then, i.e., bringing about the eternal salvation which the Jewish festival prefigured.

By commemoration, Newman means opening up our minds to "the doctrine of the Son of God dying on the Cross for us," a mystery which we cannot ever solve, though it is possible "to understand in what the Mystery consists; and that is what many men are deficient in." Such clarification is the appropriate work of this sermon, i.e., not to raise emotion by describing Christ's sufferings but to explain who He is who suffered, because that is what the mystery consists in. In doing so, "The Incarnate Son, a Sufferer and Sacrifice" is the follow-forward of the theological explanation found in "Christ the Son of God Made Man," which counteracts the twin errors of either understanding Christ "as two separate beings," or else "explaining away His Divinity altogether." Putting these prior clarifications into action, so to say, Newman states, quite simply, that "when He suffered, it was God suffering."

> Not that the Divine Nature itself could suffer, any more than our soul can see or hear; but, as the soul sees and hears through the organs of the body, so God the Son suffered *in* that human nature which He had taken to Himself and made His own . . . For when He came on earth, His manhood became as truly and personally His, as His Almighty power had been from everlasting. 6.72–3

As the sermon continues, Newman briefly recapitulates the notable features of the Passion—the soldiers, Herod, Pilate, the scourging, the crown of thorns, the mockery and insults Christ suffered while hanging between two thieves. He does so in a contracted or at least not fully elaborated manner, one which reminds readers of what they already well know, his aim being less to excite emotions than to prepare them for the theological application of those sufferings to the sermon's point, that these were in truth the sufferings of God Himself.

> Now I bid you consider that that Face, so ruthlessly smitten, was the Face of God Himself; the Brows bloody with the thorns, the sacred Body exposed to view and lacerated with the scourge, the Hands nailed to the Cross, and, afterwards, the Side pierced with the spear; it was the Blood, and the sacred Flesh, and the Hands, and the Temples, and the Side, and the Feet of God Himself, which the frenzied multitude then gazed upon. This is so fearful a thought, that when the mind first masters it, surely it will be difficult to think of any thing else; so that, while we think of it, we must pray God to temper it to us, and to give us strength to think of it rightly, lest it be too much for us. 6.74

As the sermon continues, Newman observes that surely "some great thing would result" from an occurrence so astounding as the Death of God's Son. So it has, for we owe to it our reconciliation to God through the expiation of our sins and our "new creation in holiness."

> We believe, then, that when Christ suffered on the cross, our nature suffered in Him. Human nature, fallen and corrupt, was under the wrath of God, and it was impossible that it should be restored to His favour till it had expiated its sin by suffering. Why this was necessary, we know not; but we are told expressly, that we are "all by nature children of wrath" . . . The Son of God then took our nature on Him, that in Him it might do and suffer what in itself was impossible to it. . . . In Him our sinful nature died and rose again. When it died with Him on the cross, that death was its new creation . . . for the presence of His Divinity gave it transcendent merit. 6.79

Having insisted upon the inexplicable nature of the divine revelation, Newman ends the sermon with the prayer that we not "pervert and dilute" the Faith by reasoning ourselves "out of its strictness" and reducing religion to something ordinary and commonplace, when it really involves a mystery distinct from "any thing that lies on the surface of this world."

The first sermon group of Volume 6 concludes with "The Cross of Christ the Measure of the World," a circumspective evaluation of the world and of Christianity's interpretive power within it. The epigraph "And I, if I be lifted up from the earth, will draw all men unto me," is obviously false in the sense that not all men have become Christians. Newman does not argue that they will, but that they should if they feel the need for intelligibility, because only the Cross of Christ makes sense of the world. While many men live and die without reflecting, those who do reflect find the world is "a maze and perplexity . . . without a drift." If one asks how that unsettling situation can be resolved, Newman answers that, by making consistent "all that seemed discordant and aimless," the Cross teaches us how to live. From that viewpoint, he offers a panoramic survey of human hope and its inevitable disappointment.

Juxtaposed against the world's allurements, the Cross seems to "disarrange two parts of a system" made for each other—the expectation of pleasure and the desire to embrace it—and thus it appears to ruin our prospects for happiness. Thus it seemed to Adam and Eve, who based their hopes on a "superficial view" of reality. The Cross is more efficient and direct, for it teaches without apology the same lesson the world enforces on "those who live long in it," that disappointment follows false expectations. Paradoxically, the Cross, a thing to be avoided, allows one to look deeper than "the surface of things," an illusion which is "bright only." The Cross can measure the world accurately because, overcoming disappointments, it rises up from the depths of ruined hope. In Newman's view, people have a choice either to depend upon the world and learn how baseless most human expectations are, or to learn from the Cross that those who sow in tears shall reap in joy, for "they that mourn shall be comforted."

The second sermon cluster of Volume 6 also contains seven members, all of which have been designated "Easter" sermons, although the final three have no obvious thematic connection with Easter. The other four, however, while they do not address the Resurrection directly, are entirely appropriate for the season. The first two discuss the difficulty Christians have in wholeheartedly embracing the great truths of the faith, while the other two explore Christ's Presence within those same Christians—a reality which operates beneath the radar of their earthly sens-es. "Difficulty of Realizing Sacred Privileges" opens the group with the observation that when we are told a thing, "we assent to it, we do not doubt it, but we do not feel it to be true" in this sense, that we do not understand it as "a fact which must take up a position . . . in our thoughts, and must be acted from: that is, we do not realize it." Here, Newman presents a brief sketch of the distinction between notional and real assent to truth, a subject he did not discuss fully until three decades later in his *Grammar of Assent* (1870). At this point he uses the distinc-tion to preface the difficulty of internalizing what Christ has done, pointing out that we "pass many years" learning to "rise to the understanding of our new nature," the fruit of the Resurrection.

As all our knowledge "of ourselves and of our position in the world" is gradu-ally learned, so on Easter, though we are risen with Christ, "we know it not." This reflection need not be disheartening, because little by little

> we shall give up shadows and find the substance . . . Year by year we gain something, and each Easter, as it comes, will enable us more to rejoice with heart and understanding in that great salvation which Christ then accomplished. 6.99–100

Performing our duties to God and neighbor helps to make our faith "apprehensive" of the full truth. Such is the value as well of observing liturgical seasons: "they wean us from this world" and "impress upon us the reality of the world which we see not." Yet the action whereby this takes place is too slow to provoke our awareness of the change. Newman illustrates the gradualness of the process with a georgic figure from St. Mark's Gospel, a parable in which we can recognize God as the farmer who casts seed upon the ground, after which the fertile heart "bringeth forth fruit of herself," as it were, "first the blade, then the ear, after that the full corn in the ear" (4:28).

The other Easter sermon which explores how Christians learn to live by trust-ing God rather than depending on the senses is "The Gospel Sign Addressed to Faith," which opens with the Pharisees' demands for a sign that proves Christ's authority. Newman's audience already knows that this was the demand of "an evil and adulterous generation" to whom no signs would be given except those of the Prophet Jonah, "a Sign, but not to them," and Jesus' comment that if they destroy "this temple," He will "raise it up" in three days. Both were signs whose meaning they "were to see, and not see." These reminders of unbelief have a direct bearing on Newman's audience, because the same instinct to demand some sensible indicator to verify mysterious truths is equally active in England. Approaching his readers with tact, he admits that Jesus does "expressly promise" His followers a "manifestation" of Himself, which it is

> natural, at first sight, to suppose a sensible one: and many persons understand it to be such, as if it were not more blessed to believe than to see. 6.107

Instead of being content with the ambiguous tokens that God provides, such individuals demand some "direct evidence" of God's love, an assurance "in which faith has no part."

> This is what men often conceive; not considering that whatever be the manifestation promised to Christians by our Lord, it is not likely to be more sensible and more intelligible than the great sign of His own Resurrection. Yet even that, like the miracle wrought upon Jonah, was in secret, and they who believed without seeing it were more blessed than those who saw. All this accords with what is told us about particular divine manifestations in other parts of Scripture. 6.108–9

One such manifestation addressed to faith is the manna from heaven that fed the Israelites in the desert but which in St. John's Gospel foretells the Bread of Life that Christ promises to give us, "Bread which cometh down from heaven, that a man may eat thereof and not die." Newman expressly declines to discuss Holy Communion in this sermon, except to consider "the sign in itself, as these words describe it." Here is a sign addressed not alone to the Pharisees of old but to Christians of today. As in the resurrection "His coming up from the heart of the earth was a sign for faith, not for sight," such too is "His coming down from heaven as Bread." Newman's advice therefore is not to seek for signs and wonders, since "faith only can introduce us" to God's unseen presence. The "utmost" we can do "in the way of nature is to feel after Him" like the heathen. We should not demand evidence "before believing," because "we shall gain more abundantly by believing."

In the next two sermons, the focus moves from signs to "presence," a shift initiated by "The Spiritual Presence of Christ in the Church." The question Newman investigates is What, and Where, is Christ's presence with regard to us? He answers that it is a form of spirit possession in which the risen Lord cannot be seen, because distance is required for sight and Christ is too near us to permit clear vision.

> Christ has come so close to us in the Christian Church . . . that we cannot gaze on Him or discern Him. He enters into us . . . He does not present Himself to us, but He takes us to Him. He makes us His members. Our faces are, as it were, turned from Him; we see Him not, and know not of His presence, except by faith, because He is over us and within us. 6.121–2

His Easter sermons having transitioned from our attempts to comprehend the mysteries of faith, to Christ acting in us, Newman continues by posing and answering objections against the position he has taken. For example, some will say that Christ, having promised to return after a "little while," "*has* come again, but in His Spirit; that is, His Spirit has come instead of Him." Newman responds to this view that, yes, the Spirit has come, *not* in order "to supply Christ's absence," but in order "to accomplish His presence." He has come in order "that Christ may come in His coming," because it is "through the Holy Ghost that we have communion with Father and Son." St. Paul tells us that we are "builded together for an habitation of God through the Spirit," from which we understand that the Spirit does not take Christ's place in the soul, but "secures that place to Christ."

Another like objection is that "we are not in Christ's presence, else we should be conscious of it," yet it should be self-evident that we are not so conscious. Says Newman, with a view to meeting this objection,

> let us turn to the account of His appearances to His disciples after the Resurrection, which are most important, first, as showing that such an unconscious communion with Christ is possible; next, that it is likely to be the sort of communion now granted to us, from the circumstance that in that period of forty days after the Resurrection, He began to be in that relation towards His Church, in which He still is, and probably intended to intimate to us thereby what His presence with us is now. 6.131

Christ's presence is quite different after His resurrection than before. After it, He "came and went as He pleased," abruptly appearing, disappearing, passing through doors and presenting Himself in a manner such that His close friends did not immediately know Him. This new mode of presence is evident in the experience of the disciples going to Emmaus. They could not recognize Him, because "their hearts seem to have been holden (if we may use the expression) as well as their eyes." They were surely receiving impressions from Christ as they walked along listening to Him, but they were unable to realize who He was, except in retrospect after He had disappeared. Focusing our attention, Newman says, "Let us observe, too, *when* it was that their eyes were opened."

> Here we are suddenly introduced to the highest and most solemn Ordinance of the Gospel [the Eucharist] . . . For so it was ordained, that Christ should not be both seen and known at once; first He was seen, then He was known. Only by faith is He known to be present; He is not recognized by sight. When He opened His disciples' eyes, He at once vanished. He removed His visible presence, and left but a memorial of Himself. He vanished from sight that He might be present in a sacrament; and in order to connect His visible presence with His presence invisible, He for one instant manifested Himself to their open eyes; manifested Himself . . . while He passed from His hiding-place of sight without knowledge, to that of knowledge without sight. 6.132–3

In summation, Newman asserts that while Christ has promised to be with us even to the end time, he is not present with us "locally and sensibly," but in our hearts and through the perceptions of faith. Like the disciples going the road to Emmaus, we too will "on looking back" realize that He has been with us. "Such is the Day of the Lord in which we find ourselves" (1270).

The last of the four Easter sermons which is pertinent to that feast, "The Eucharistic Presence" is a meditation on Chapter 6 of St. John's Gospel, in which Jesus solemnly and insistently tells the crowd that He is "the bread which came down from heaven," while unbelieving Jews "murmured at him" (6:41). Newman calls Holy Communion "the greatest and highest" of all the Church's Sacramental mysteries because Christ "is in it spiritually present."

> We call His presence in this Holy Sacrament a spiritual presence, not as if "spiritual" were but a name or mode of speech, and He were really absent, but by way of expressing that He who is present there can neither be seen nor heard; that He cannot be approached or ascertained by any of the senses. . . . How this is, of course is a mystery. All we know or need know is that He *is* given to us, and that in the Sacrament of Holy Communion. 6.136–7

The perennial objection to a literal understanding of Christ's assertions is that they obviously cannot be true. And the perennial rejection of His words is accomplished by reducing them to a figurative expression, any substitution that does not insult natural perception. Newman objects to such dismissive reduction by reminding his audience that it is as faithless "to overlook signs when given as to ask for them when withheld." Refusing to believe Christ, the Jews "were but imitating their ancestors in the wilderness," who ignored Moses and searched on the seventh day hoping for manna they would not find. These ancestors went expecting "mere food," ignoring its having been "miraculously given" as a token of their "immediate dependence" upon the Giver. Their unbelief is identical to that of Newman's thoughtless contemporaries, who "come to the Lord's Table without awe, admiration, hope," losing the benefit of Holy Communion by not believing it to be an "invisible work of power." This is the corruption of belief St. Paul warns the Corinthians about, their "not *discerning* the Lord's Body."

In this sermon, Newman develops at considerable length the parallel between the miracle of the loaves and Holy Communion, calling the former "a kind of protection of the mystery of the Eucharist against objections with which men are wont to assail it; as, for instance, that it is impossible." Feeding the many with a small basket of bread is unlike Christ's other miracles, which are "intelligible though supernatural." That is, while we do not understand how a blind man's eyes are healed or how the dead can be raised to life, we do know what those statements mean. But "what *is meant* by saying that the loaves fed five thousand persons?" Precisely the same objection is raised against "the mystery of Christ's Presence in

Holy Communion." In both of these mysterious actions the identical procedure is followed: the taking of bread, blessing the bread or giving thanks, breaking it, and distributing it. In short, "The feeding of the multitude with the loaves, interprets the Lord's Supper." He who multiplied the loaves is, as He said, "the *true* Manna, the *true* Bread that came down from heaven."

> It is not God's mercy, or favour, or imputation; it is not a state of grace, or the promise of eternal life, or the privileges of the Gospel, or the new covenant; it is not, much less, the doctrine of the Gospel, or faith in that doctrine; but it is what our Lord says it is, the gift of His own precious Body and Blood, really given, taken, and eaten as the manna might be (though in a way unknown), at a certain particular time, and a certain particular spot; namely, . . . at the time and spot when and where the Holy Communion is celebrated. 6.143–4

At the midpoint of Volume 6, Newman has inserted as "Easter" sermons three reflective sermons which do not have a direct bearing upon that liturgical season, or any other. However, they have been appropriately included because all three deal with faith, which spreads its radiance over the entire Sacramental Season, whose goal is celebrating faith. These three sermons—"Faith the Title for Justification," "Judaism of the Present Day," and "The Fellowship of the Apostles"—all address the question of whether and how the dissenters, the English sectarians, might be saved. The problem in Newman's view is that God wills that salvation come through the Church which Christ established, but the dissenters are outside of it, because they neither observe its ordinances nor accept its Creeds, without errors. This investigative focus is the probable reason for their having been included in the volume.

The particular value of these sermons for students of Newman is that they provide a window onto the alteration of emphasis in his pastoral thought between 1835 and 1840, the five year span between hard-hitting attacks on theological degeneration in Volumes 2 and 3, and these gentler sermons. They reveal that Newman has arrived at a more sympathetic understanding of the salvation prospects of those he still considers separated from the Church.

Changing opinions can be easy or difficult, depending on how energetically they were embraced, and for how long. Most would agree that a reflective person's position on any complex subject typically begins with some relatively naïve presumptions, which then feel the intellectual pressure of current thinking on that subject, which includes views that one may think right, or wrong, or simply wonder about. In the evaluation process that occurs, thinking finds its rest in a stable balancing act that is called one's position on the subject. New information or the passing of time may require a modification of earlier views, leading to subtle alterations or even total reversal of convictions no longer confidently embraced. Newman's beliefs are stable but open to alteration. One sees it in his reply to James Stephen's charge that he was unfair to the Evangelicals. Already in 1835, at the high point of his attack on theological error, Newman shows an ability to qualify, which permits him to rethink the sectarian question five years later. Answering Stephen, he says

> Nothing I believe in my Sermons is against them except so far forth as they hold certain opinions . . . Against the *spirit* of their school certainly I have spoken strongly; and, while I believe (as I do now, whether rightly or wrongly,) that that spirit tends to liberalism and Socinianism, I ever must. This is the reason for my strong language, my fear of a system of doctrine which eats out the heart of godliness, where truer and holier instincts do not exclude it from producing its legitimate results. *L & D*, V, 31–2

In his "sectarian" sermons, the spirit of rationalism that Newman objected to in Whately, Hampden and Milman is not a factor. Therefore, his anxieties concerning doctrinal error can loosen, freeing his mind to consider freshly the "truer and holier instincts" of faith-filled Christians outside of the Anglican communion.

"The Fellowship of the Apostles," which Newman places in final position, was written before its companions. It is a draft version of ideas which, by October, 1839, he had begun seriously considering. The sermon's tentative nature is clear from its title, which does not state a conclusion, but rather presents a subject to be examined. He is less concerned here to persuade than to lay out evidence and to test arguments by formulating them. As if thinking his way forward, Newman says that before the Gospel "was received," those who did not interfere with the Apostles helped them, but later on, the same parties impeded the Apostles' work, though nothing had changed except the degree of success the new system had had. As a probative instance, he says that "once the Church was set up" John the Baptist's disciples, doubtless people of good faith, had to submit to the Church "and leave the sect." This reflection does not provide any larger insight but simply examines the evidence to see what further argument might be latent there. More substantively pertinent is the observation that there are many in England "who neither have themselves separated from the Church, nor opposed it," which seems to be an excellent reason for not attacking them. What is Newman to think of the sectarians? His first step towards discovering what he now believes is to consider the facts of the case.

> Many sects and parties in this country are of long standing; many men are born in them; many men have had no opportunity of knowing the truth. Again, it may so happen that they are exerting themselves for the cause of Christ in places where the Church is unknown, or where it does not extend itself. And, moreover, it may be so that they have upon them many consolatory proofs of seriousness and earnestness, of a true love for Christ, and desire to obey Him and not to magnify themselves. Here, then, our Lord seems to say, "Forbid them not in their preaching." 6.204

This text is powerfully reminiscent of St. Peter's similar reversal when, follow-ing the trance wherein he saw "a great sheet" being lowered, full of animals which Jews considered unclean, he finally understood the vision: "God hath shewed me that I should not call any man common or unclean," for everyone who "feareth him, and worketh righteousness, is accepted with him" (*Acts* 10:11–35). It seems evi-dent that Newman shared with St. Peter both the discomfiture and the relief of moving towards the light of better understanding. Nevertheless, he does not aban-don his prior views, because, while advising his audience "to be kind and tolerant to all Christian bodies" who in faith labor in the same cause, he insists upon the caveat that they do so "*as far* as these latter do not actively interfere" with the Anglican Church "or oppose her doctrine, which, alas! will too often be the case."

This closing flick of semi-petulant complaint suggests that Newman is embar-rassed to find his pen write such stuff as this, as though fearing he might inadver-tently surrender integrity by finding common cause with the sectarians. Yet he does not reverse his course, but moves gradually forward to the point that, by January, 1841, he is able to entitle his follow-on sermon "Faith the Title for Justification." Although Jesus says "Many shall come from the east and the west" and claim their place beside the Patriarchs, the New Testament makes it clear that faith is "not enough." It is the introduction which leads towards "other conditions," as shown by the case of the Ethiopian Eunuch, who "had a title to justification" on account of his faith but "was baptized in order to receive it." Faith provides the "warrant" that God "will justify" a man. On the one hand, Newman insists upon the princi-ple that "the grace of the Gospel is lodged in a divinely appointed body, and spreads from *it*." On the other hand, while those external to the Church are not *in* it and are therefore excluded from the immediate source of grace, in Newman's position "we may humbly, yet confidently say, that where there is true faith, there justification shall be; there it is promised, it is due, it is coming, somehow, some-while." But when? At Christ's second coming? At the moment the sectarian dies? By some "extraordinary dispensation" we know nothing about? It is impossible to say. Nevertheless, "every one that calleth on the Name of the Lord" in faith "shall be saved."

"Judaism of the Present Day" bolsters the argument of "Faith the Title . . ." by advancing a relevant parallel, i.e., that those outside the Church who have lively faith are in the condition of the Jewish Patriarchs, who "died in faith, not having received the promises, but having seen them from afar off" (*Heb* 11:13). The par-allel holds true because one may have faith, yet "still not be justified" because the time of one's justification has not arrived, even though in God's secret counsels one may be "ordained unto it." Like the Patriarchs, many in England are "in that intermediate, provisional" place where Anglicans put them, "who hold that the Sacraments of the Church are . . . necessary for justification" (1300). Here we meet a second reason why Newman appropriately placed these three sermons in Volume 6. Not only because the leitmotif of the volume is faith, but also because it discusses the Sacramental Season, which bears upon the sectarians in the way Newman has just explained. In closing, Newman reverses the same paradigm he has just advanced, so that it accuses Anglicans of little faith. "Is it wonderful," he asks, that those in the Church who stop receiving Holy Communion and "rest in faith" for their salvation should "fall back into a state like the Jews?"

Ascension is represented by four sermons, the first two of them pep talks. Relatively brief, both rouse their audience to exert themselves in the good fight, which is an important function of the sermon form, even if Newman's are usually more intellectually vigorous. "Rising With Christ" encourages Christians to seek heavenly things and not be "possessed and absorbed" by the world. The dominant image is the mountaintop, which lends itself to Newman's setting Moses on Sinai and Jesus in the Transfiguration against the flat-landers Pilate, Herod and the Pharisees, who represent the souls milling around the mountain's base, oblivious to the "marvellous system" advancing under the world's "veil." One guesses that the sermon is more effective as heard than as read, its attraction being the glow of excited feeling. Either way, Newman adjures his audience to "mount up" from old Adam's grave and set their affection on "things above."

"Warfare the Condition of Victory" is similar, for it applies to Newman's audience the Apostles' summons to spread the good news, when, Christ having ascended, they "worshipped Him, and returned to Jerusalem with great joy." The theme is bold action on behalf of God's kingdom. After wondering why the Apostles were so elated when they might have been saddened by losing Christ again so soon after the resurrection, Newman surmises that such rejoicing was "the high temper of the brave and noble-minded, who have faced danger and are prepared for it." That is the activity the sermon hopes to foster, i.e., preparing oneself for one's eventual self-sacrifice by facing it "in idea" beforehand. Using the typology of parallel situations, Newman reflects that as Moses invested forty years turning "a timid nation" into a people trained for "the task of conquering the promised land," and as Christ during the forty days before His ascension taught the Apostles to be "bold and patient," not cowards, so his own audience will succeed only if they have been well prepared for the fight. Nor does this Oxford academic shrink from using something akin to locker-room exhortation to raise their enthusiasm.

And so down to this very time, when faith has well-nigh failed, first one and then another have been called out to exhibit before the Great King. It is as though all of us were allowed to stand around His Throne at once, and He called on first this man, and then that, to take up the chant by himself, each in his turn having to repeat the melody which his brethren have before gone through . . . or as if it were some trial of strength, or of agility [and] we in

> succession . . . were actors in the pageant. Such is our state . . . O let not your foot slip, or
> your eye be false, or your ear dull, or your attention flagging! . . . be bold. 6.230

As Christ rose to glory by suffering, as did the Apostles in imitation of Him, so must all Christians. It is written "through much tribulation we must enter into the kingdom of God." Or as the sermon's title expresses the same thought, warfare is "the Condition of Victory."

In contrast to the pep talks which precede them, the final two Ascension sermons are a thoughtful investigation of time in relation to faith, an investigation prompted by the question, if "this same Jesus, which is taken up from you into heaven" will return to earth again (*Acts*, 1:11), how long is that going to take? When millenia creep by and Christians are disappointed in their expectation, how long can they continue expecting Him while holding their breath? Newman's answer draws upon a distinction that Paul Ricoeur calls "the polarity between the time of consciousness and the time of world," that is, "the discordance between the time of the world and lived time" (*Time and Narrative*, III, 131–2). That distinction is forever being overtaken by the quasi-tactile inevitability of clock time, which shoulders aside the more private reality of lived time. Now both the worldly man and the Christian have their distinctive human experience in the psychological dimension of consciousness, the interior time sense in which Macbeth, meditating on the emptiness of an existence where time is bondage, muses that "Tomorrow, and tomorrow, and tomorrow/ Creeps in this petty pace from day to day" (V, vii, 19–20). The Christian has hope, Macbeth none, yet the faithful waiting for Christ's coming can apprehend the futility that Macbeth experiences. However, the Christian has the duty of awaiting His return, something the natural man despairs of because the world's clock keeps ticking inexorably on, while the light of newly forming solar systems shines brighter than Gospel promises.

The first of the final two Ascension sermons, "Waiting for Christ," begins by posing the objection that one cannot "ever be expecting" something which has been long delayed, since "what fails to come, you give up." Newman begins his answer by discussing the phenomenon of time during the ages when Christ was yet to come, setting that sense of time in contrast to time's conduct following His advent. Before, a system of revelation was gradually unfolding through the successive installments of prophecy, a cumulative process which shaped the manner in which time "was measured out by believing minds." But after Christ had come, no further revelation could be expected, and no greater priest would appear, so that time became "the last time." Chronological time, linear in its movement, was displaced in the Gospel schema by circular time, which turns upon a stable center.

> Up to Christ's coming in the flesh, the course of things ran straight towards that end, nearing it by every step; but now . . . [it] runs, not towards the end, but along it, and on the brink

of it; and is at all times equally near that great event, which, did it run towards it, it would at once run into. 6.241

Christ is "ever at our doors," as near on the day of His ascension as today, but not nearer now than then, nor any nearer "when He comes than now." What St. Paul calls "the present distress" is the time of Christianity in the world, a time which is "ever close upon the next world, and resolves itself into it." Clearly, time has been changed from a measure of temporal sequence to the substance of our interior experience. In Paul Ricoeur's terms, "lived time" has displaced "the time of the world." That is to say, time has been interiorized so that it becomes the extended present, or in other words, the psychological activity of "joining together having-been, coming-towards, and making-present" (III, 133). Or, as St. Augustine would put it, the "now" of the past which resides in memory and the "now" of the future entrusted to expectation, are entwined within the "now" of present intuition. The better to characterize the feeling tone of waiting for Christ's return when it is constantly delayed, Newman offers a series of similitudes:

> As when a man is given over, he may die any moment, yet lingers; as an implement of war may any moment explode, and must at some time; as we listen for a clock to strike, and at length it surprises us; as a crumbling arch hangs, we know not how, and is not safe to pass under; so creeps on this feeble weary world, and one day, before we know where we are, it will end. 6.241

In all times of the Gospel, we stand beneath the Cross and receive Christ's blessings "fresh from it." This is true even though, "historically speaking," time has moved on and necessitated "outward forms" by which we can approach His blessings "sacramentally," which is the particular focus of Volume 6. All of this, says Newman, "witnesses to the duty both of remembering and of looking out for Christ," a duty which teaches Christians to live in faith "as if He had not left us," but also in hope, "as if He had returned to us." Christians should meditate on Christ's life in the Gospels "not as a history" narrating things remote from us, "but as if a recollection" of events which retain their immediacy within lived time.

Having described time's intricate nature in the Gospel system, Newman directs his argument to the objections which might be urged against waiting for Christ, as for instance that doing so is "extravagant in its very idea," and that it becomes "a superstitious weakness" because one's mind begins to "fancy" signs of His coming, with the result that "imagination takes the place of faith, and things visible and earthly take the place of Scripture." However, Newman argues to the contrary that wars and rumors thereof, along with natural disasters and the condition of the sun, moon and stars, are "the very signs" which Christ tells us will precede His coming, and it is surely better "to be wrong in watching, than not to watch at all." Moreover, not only is it a mistake to call watching for Christ superstitious, but on the contrary watching draws forth spiritual perceptions which otherwise would not be activated. Further, Scripture endorses the active interpretation of all the events which we see around us as "tokens and revelations" of the divine purpose. One could argue, as Newman himself does in other contexts, that the world is "a deceitful veil" between the soul and God, "yet certainly so it is, that in spite of the world's evil, after all, He is in it and speaks through it, though not loudly."

> His voice is so low, and the world's din is so loud, and His signs are so covert, and the world is so restless, that it is [hard to hear] . . . what He says. 6.248

Newman's concluding move in this sermon is to refocus sharply away from the time of the world, to lived time, the dimension of spiritual awareness which provides the quiet interior evidences of prayers having been answered, dreams having reliably led us on, and similar "presages remarkably fulfilled in the event." On the basis of evidence of this nature which the religious heart perceives, Christians

> come to believe, and they begin to have a sort of faith in the Divine meaning of the accidents (as they are called) of life, and a readiness to take impressions from them, which may easily become excessive, and which whether excessive or not, is sure to be ridiculed by the world at large as superstitious. 6.249

God does not speak to us through the events of our lives so clearly that we could use such evidence to persuade others, but it is enough to give us that modicum of certainty which can "raise our minds in awe towards Him." Does this amount to superstition? Not in Newman's judgment, for the man of faith "does not come to the world" or even probe his own experience "for a revelation—-he has one already."

"Waiting for Christ" did not exhaust Newman's thinking on the subject, which spilled over into "Subjection of the Reason and Feelings to the Revealed Word," written within a week or two of the earlier sermon. His focus changes by a certain broadening, but the investigation remains the same. "Subjection of the Reason . . ." announces its theme in its epigraph, " . . . bringing into captivity every thought to the obedience of Christ." Once again, Newman commences the sermon by stating an objection he will oppose, namely, that we cannot live as if Christ's coming would occur soon, when our reason tells us that that event "is not probable," nor can we "make ourselves feel" that it *is* when judgment tells us it is not. Newman counters this objection, supported by reason and emotion, with the "great principle" of Christian duty, that of subjecting "the whole mind" to the law of God. The natural man does not easily surrender evaluative faculties he constantly depends upon, but Newman's view is that faith requires precisely that surrender.

Having clarified what is at issue, Newman initiates his argument proper by denying that our feelings are "only moved" by reason, since nothing is so common as for reason to go one way, our feelings another. And because it is not impossible for the sinful and irreligious "to like what their reason tells them they should not like," neither is it impossible for religious persons "to desire, expect, and hope what their reason is unequal to approve and accept." Moreover, when a robbery, murder or fire occurs in a man's own neighborhood, he will feel it more probable that he may be robbed and murdered, or his house consumed by fire, than is statistically likely, says Newman. His fears overcome his reason. The kind of instinctive terror which overcomes the fearful man, if the emotion be reversed and differently applied, provides Christians a situational strategy: if the likelihood of Christ's coming seems to you very remote, you can dwell upon the possibility that it *is* likely, as others dwell on the possibility of their being robbed or murdered. "Open your mind to it," Newman advises. "Treat that chance just as you so often treat the chance of fire, or peril by sea." Or the chance of robbery, because when Jesus says He will come like a thief in the night, He offers a Scriptural precedent for arousing the emotion of expectation, even in the absence of any evidence beyond the Divine Word that it will happen, and happen suddenly.

The second step of the argument is to remind readers of the relationship between faith and reason, i.e., that faith is "an acceptance of things unseen . . . *beyond* the determinations of calculation and experience." True faith "cares not for the measure of probabilities." It does not ask whether something is "more or less likely," nor "regard *degrees* of evidence." Reason left to itself would insist that we have faith only "according to the evidence," such that the more evidence we have, the "more firm" our faith. But religious faith is different. It "accepts the word of God as firmly" on the evidence that is given to us, "as if that evidence were doubled." God has given enough, faith "does not ask for more." Thus, there is no justification for being reluctant to "wait for Him perseveringly" even if the signs that point towards His coming "disappoint us, and reason desponds." Reason is beyond its competence here.

> We cannot tell in such a matter what is more probable and what is not; we can but attempt what we are told to do. And *that* we can do: we can direct and fashion our feelings according to His Word, and leave the rest to Him. 6.260

Newman's third move is to answer the objection that the waiting Christian cannot live effectively in the world because he will have permanently distracted himself through constant anticipation of an unlikely event. He does so by pointing out that, just as we have a duty to bring certain things before our minds and "contemplate them much more vividly than reason by itself" would approve, we have on the other hand a duty to "put away from us" other things—not dwell upon, not realize them—even though they present themselves before us. Here, Newman would seem tacitly to adopt the remark of Milton's Satan, that "the mind is its own place" and governs that territory. For instance, while a talented or holy person may recognize his own performance and gifts, he need not therefore become conceited and vain about what he recognizes as true. Such a person can refuse to dwell on what is potentially dangerous to his character, lest he be puffed up and attribute to himself everything he is and has. Well then, Newman argues, "what men omit to do when the doing is a duty, they can surely also omit to do in cases when omission is a duty." Thus the sermon gives examples of this truth, that Christian character "is formed by a rule higher than that of calculation and reason," a rule which "transcends the anticipations and criticisms of ordinary men." As for the Christian's acting effectively in the world, even though he understands that when Christ comes he will "cut things short," he also understands that in the designs of Providence "our efforts and beginnings" may be as fruitful as "the most successful accomplishment." No inconsistency exists between our watching for Christ and our working in the world, since we can work without setting our hearts on whatever it is we have to do. The only sin would be loving our work so inordinately that we cannot bear to part with it. "The test of our faith lies in being able to fail without disappointment."

Three of the four Pentecost sermons in Volume 6 focus upon the "enduring," "stately" and "ornamental" churches of Christendom, though no one of them is singled out by being named. It is the phenomenon, not any particular structure, which is Newman's subject. Of these three sermons, the first two are strikingly similar to "The Kingdom of the Saints," the paired Pentecost sermons featured in volume 2. These, memorable for their enthusiastic range and triumphal confidence, present the evidence that Providential design directly controlled the astonishing success of those few unlearned fishermen who established the Gospel throughout the known world, rapidly and against great odds. The story of the Church's dissemination following the Holy Ghost's descent at Pentecost, begun in the pair of earlier sermons, is continued in Volume 6 by "The Gospel Palaces" and "The Visible Temple." These cover a somewhat later span of time and redirect attention from Providence to the architectural vigor of those spirit-filled Christians who, once the time had become ripe to sustain their efforts, filled the earth with "magnificent" churches.

These sermons necessarily examine a later time because during the early centuries of the Church, Christ's subjects worshipped in forests at night, or in catacombs, while "the great people" of the day fashioned above ground the stately tombs that would house their remains. This echoes Christ's history, for He began His counter-occupation of the world from underneath the ground. Poor-Boy-Makes-Good has always been an attractive story line, and thus it was with Mary's Son. "He came in the dark, in the dark night was He born, in a cave under ground." However, "He came into that cave to leave it," and to take His newly-freed companions along with Him. Says Newman, "He laid Himself on the damp earth in the cold night, a light shining in a dark place, till by the virtue that went out from Him, He should create a Temple worthy of His Name." First and above all, this new creation is the spiritual temple built of the living stones of redeemed souls. Yet those same souls were to celebrate their joyful affection for Christ after their release from captivity by erecting visible temples everywhere. "Pass a few generations, and the whole face of things is changed; the earth is covered with His Temples; as it has been for ages. Go where you will, you find the eternal mountains hewn and fashioned into shrines where He may dwell, who was an outcast in the days of His flesh."

But like the "eternal mountains," Christ's triumphal reclamation of the world He once created is characterized by gradualism and proxy-agency. That is, recovery of the territory usurped by Satan is not immediate, but is instead a slow accumulation over time. Further, that divine action has been sub-contracted to Christ's proxies in the world, i.e., the members of His mystical body, the communion of saints. It is God's victory at one remove, as the natural geological phenomenon of pressure plates moving in opposite directions lifted those eternal mountains, not directly but independently of their Creator. The great work, the heavy lifting which only the Son of God could perform, has been completed, but the challenge remains. And therefore, while the centrality of Christ's salvation is evident, so too on the other hand, its gradualism and its proxy character are clear. No one will deny that

> a great object of Christ's coming was to subdue this world, to assert His rights as its Master, and to destroy the usurped dominion of the enemy, to show Himself to all men and to take possession. 6.283

Yet on the other hand, that *taking* of possession is largely the responsibility of His field troops in the world. His success through gradualism and proxy action is expressed by Newman's applying to His faithful followers Jesus' figures of the mustard seed and the leaven, both of which imply, by figural redeployment, Christ's aims advancing through the independent actions of those whose hearts beat in time with His own. Thus when Newman says *He*, he means His spiritual presence within us.

> He is that Mustard-tree which was destined silently to spread and overshadow all lands; He is that Leaven which was secretly to make its way through the mass of human opinion and institutions till the whole was leavened. His gracious purpose was to make them one, and that by making earth like heaven. 6.283

Focusing on one facet of the proxy action entrusted to Christians in the field, Newman in "The Gospel Palaces" and "The Visible Temple" presents the building of churches as an act of divine worship. "All ye who take part in the building of a Church, know that you have been admitted to the truest symbol of God's eternity." The effect of such participation is to expand an individual's life expectancy, since "faith alone lengthens a man's existence, and makes him, in his own feelings, live in the future and in the past." The Christian "throws himself fearlessly upon the future" because he sets his hand to a work that he cannot expect to finish. He begins "what others must accomplish." Nowhere is this more palpably true than in the construction of Churches, which requires both singleness of purpose and long-sustained communal determination. How were the great cathedrals raised? Cooperatively, during many generations.

> One age would build a Chancel, and another a Nave, and a third would add a Chapel, and a fourth a Shrine, and a fifth a Spire. By little and little the work of grace went forward. 6.275

While the thrust of these two sermons is a celebration of God's work going forward in human hands, Newman tempers his enthusiasm somewhat in occasional lamentations that the Christian giants of old have given way to the pygmies of his own day, for his century was not a great age of Church construction. Setting aside the flurry of action aimed at replacing the sacred buildings destroyed in the Great Fire of London during the late 1660's, the English had long been living on the stone legacy of earlier days, the marvellous structures of his own Oxford being a case in point. In the former age, the work of raising Churches went forward; now, it has stopped. And hence Newman's bittersweet reflection that, although they are no longer being built, many remain.

> O happy they, who, in a sorrowful time, avail themselves of this bond of communion with the Saints of old and with the Universal Church! O wise and dutiful, who, when the world has robbed them of so much, set the more account upon what remains! We have not lost all, while we have the dwelling-places of our forefathers. 6.279

What more sorrowful time, from Newman's point of view, than that in which Milman interprets the history of Christianity and Dr. Hampden occupies the official chair of theological teaching in Oxford University?

The third of the sermons in Volume 6 which are focused on Churches, "Offerings for the Sanctuary," moves away from celebration towards Newman's most habitual rhetorical form, argumentation. He begins by advancing the Old Testament precedent for beautifying the Lord's Temple, quoting from *Isaiah*: "For brass I will bring gold, and for iron I will bring silver, and for wood brass, and for stones iron; thou shalt call thy walls Salvation, and thy gates Praise" (60:17–18). The connection between ornament and worship is important for Newman because the position he will oppose is that decorating church interiors is nothing but an external form, the ersatz holiness practiced by the whited-sepulcre Pharisees whom Jesus condemned. Quite to the contrary, "If it be said that some of these expressions are figurative" and should not be understood literally, that interpretation does not argue against ornamentation, since "the materials literally denoted may be suitably used in its fulfilment" unless such use is "actually forbidden," which it is not. Further, gold, silver and brass "do not cease to be figures because they are actually present as well as spoken of. Real gold is as much a figure in the Church, as the mention of it is such in Scripture." The opposite position is held by many people, those who have come to think that "the more homely and familiar their worship is, the more spiritual it becomes."

The procedure Newman adopts to lay out his argument is to present a parallel between the beautifying of Churches and being well washed and neatly dressed—turning against his objectors the proverb which they have always heard but not understood, that cleanliness is next to godliness. His rhetorical opponent objects, first, that what God requires is "a clean heart, not a neat appearance." Newman answers by saying duty requires both, because "inward exactness and sanctity" tend to "*show* themselves" in a right appearance. Next, the objector complains that persons who are neat and decent in appearance "had often very bad tempers," and they made "a *point* of being neat" and quarrelled with "every one who interfered" with them. Newman replies, "If so, it was to be lamented," but still it is right to be neat and wrong to be slovenly, because "exactness within showed itself in exactness without." The objector's subsequent complaint is that "propriety in dress became love of finery" which makes persons who are meticulous about their appearance "vain." In part, Newman agrees: "All this ought not to be," because "vanity is a great sin"; yet those considerations do not prove that "neatness and decency" have no claim to praise, but "that love of finery was perilous, and vanity sinful."

Newman next applies the argument he has been laying out to the case of beautifying churches: "as is neatness and decency in an individual, such is decoration in a Church," and as we ought to be offended by slovenliness in dress, "so ought we to be offended at disorder and neglect in our Churches." Notice that the terms of the argument have changed, ostentatious vanity having been displaced by conspicuous disrespect shown to a holy place. In truth, making "the beauty of holiness visible" by decorating the sanctuary does not reduce religion into mere external show, but is "natural" and "consistent" in those whose religious lives are genuine. What is deeply offensive in those who pretend is "most necessary" in people who are sincere. But Newman's argument reaches well beyond interior decorating, even of a church. His crucial point is that though we must begin with the heart, we must not end there.

> We must not give up this visible world, as if it came from the evil one. It is our duty to change it into the kingdom of heaven. [In this regard,] they who rejoice *with* their brethren in their

common salvation, and desire to worship together, *build a place* to worship in, and they build it as the *expression* of their feelings, of their mutual love, of their common reverence. They build a building which will, as it were, speak; which will profess and confess Christ their Saviour; which will herald forth His death and passion at first sight; which will remind all who enter that we are saved by His cross, and must bear our cross after Him. 6.304–5

The sermon ends by responding to a final objection to the parallel Newman has laid out between personal dress and church ornament, i.e., that "decoration is wrong when it is intentional and studied," since those who are anxious about their dress are either vain or are becoming so. In answer, those who make much of their dress contemplate themselves, while in attending to the "ceremonial of religion" we are contemplating God. Although it is baseless in itself, the objection is worth examining since doing so helps to unmask the disingenuousness of those who so argue, for

it is the way of the world to be most sensitively jealous of over-embellishment in the worship of God, while it has no scruples or misgivings whatever at an excess of splendour and magnificence in its own apparel, houses, furniture, equipages, and establishments. . . . It is the way of us Englishmen, who are the richest people upon earth, to lay out our wealth upon ourselves; and when the thought crosses our minds, if it ever does, that such an application of God's bounties is unworthy those who are named after Him who was born in a stable, and died upon the Cross, we quiet them by asking, "What is the use of all the precious things which God has given us, if we may not enjoy them?" 6.307

Thus what was initially represented as a Puritan preference for simplicity and sincerity in religion in contrast to the gaudy emptiness of the Romanist sympathizers is at sermon's end unmasked as simple greed, which refuses to be called by its proper name.

The Trinity Sunday sermons which conclude Volume 6 complete Newman's two-volume celebration of the liturgical seasons. Trinity is different from the feasts which precede it because Christmas, Easter, Ascension, Pentecost and the others focus upon what God has done for us, but Trinity Sunday celebrates God as He exists within Himself. The Divine Nature, beyond our capacity to comprehend, is a mystery that cannot be ameliorated, lessened, or encroached upon by the mind's best efforts to understand how there can be three Persons, yet one God. The doctrine thwarts our investigation at every turn, for after the mind has done its best to clarify the precise content of what has been revealed, the essence of the mystery, the Reality itself, is beyond the limited reach of our intellects. So Trinity Sunday is necessarily a celebration of the incomprehensible reality of God's being insofar as it has been revealed, a mystery to be accepted solely on faith in God's word.

This focus upon faith is evident in the titles of the three sermons, i.e., "*Faith Without Demonstration*," "The *Mystery* of the Holy Trinity" and "Peace in

Believing." The first of these addresses the error that those people fall into who suppose that, because the doctrine of the Trinity "is maintained as being in Scripture," they therefore "have a right to say that they will not believe it till it is proved to *them* from Scripture." These mistaken persons presume that only a "rational belief" is acceptable to God and that any other mode of acceptance of the doctrine "is blind and superstitious." Yet if God, Who is not bound to do so, chooses to reveal His own nature, which He has done, that revelation *can* be accepted only upon faith, because no other way is open to us. The best aspect of this sermon is Newman's demonstration of the absurdity of his opponent's position, which utilizes an extended analogy between faith in God's Word and the binding language of the English Law.

Were Newman's objector to find himself in a potential dispute with the Laws of England, he would humble himself before that law because "loss of property or imprisonment" could result if he broke it, and the meaning of particular laws is "not always obvious to common sense"—that being the balance upon which he would weigh the reasonableness of the Trinity. Reluctant to "act upon his own private notions," he would "consult someone skilled in the law," not because he is suspicious of the law books but because he feels "how much is at stake" and is not willing to "trust *himself*."

> He cannot afford, in such a case, to indulge his love of argument, disputation, and criticism. No, this love of argument can only be indulged in a case in which we have no fears. It is reserved for religious subjects. Such subjects differ from all other practical subjects, as being those on which the world feels free to speculate, because it does not *fear*. 6.331

The world can assert that it will not believe "'till I see proof in Scripture for believing,'" although it is too prudent to extend this and say "'I will not believe lawyers till I understand the law.'" Why? Because the world "sees clearly and feels deeply that the law of the land is a real power, and that to come into collision with it is a real disaster." Newman's advice to the contrary is to suppress potential objections, to not ask "jealously and coldly for strict arguments" (an irrelevant demand because the Trinity is a mystery), and generously accept the evidence which we have. That, after all, is how we have come to believe that there is a God, whatever be His nature. The voice within us which "assures us" that there is something higher than this world is not something we can "analyze" or "define," yet this yearning of our nature is our crucial evidence for believing that God exists. We ought therefore to "exercise a similar faith, as regards the Mysteries of Revelation."

The second member of the final sermon group, "The Mystery of the Holy Trinity," discusses the doctrine in the context of the objections raised against it, whether by misbelievers or puzzled Christians. Although the doctrine is frequently objected to as obscure, Newman points out to the contrary that the Athanasian creed, which presents it, does not employ "dark language, and difficult speculation," for no sentences can be "more simple," no statements "more precise" than those found therein. The difficulty lies not in the words, but in the mystery of God's being, "which no wording can remove or explain." It would thus be folly in Newman to explain the doctrine, but helpful to state its meaning. The most engaging and challenging portion of his effort to "state" the doctrine is the extended illustration he develops based on Scripture's "material images" of the "eye" of God and the "ear" of God to provide his audience a gropingly analogous sense of how God could be all wisdom, all love, all justice, and yet neither consist of multiple faculties nor be divisible into parts. We do not know what the consequence would be of Newman's audience having their bodies be made "spiritual" because "it is beyond us." Yet since a spirit has no parts, one can conceive the organs of the human body being "all one, though all distinct still." Following this line of conjecture, Newman says that

> As a body need not be supposed to lose eye and hand by becoming spiritual, but its organs might exist in it as truly as before, because it was a body, but in a new manner, because it was spiritual . . . so may we suppose that though . . . God is a Spirit and One, yet He may be also a Trinity; not as if that Trinity were a name only, or stood for three manifestations, or qualities, or attributes, or relations . . . but that, as in that body which had become spiritual, eye and hand would not be abstractions after the change . . . in like manner I say, . . . the Eternal Three are worshipped by the Catholic Church as distinct, yet One . . . the Three Persons being distinct from each other, not merely in name, or by human abstraction, but in very truth, as truly as a fountain is distinct from the stream which flows from it, or the roots of a tree from its branches. 6.351–2

The Trinity is a founding doctrine of Christianity because Christ sent His Apostles to teach and baptize in the Name of the Triune God, and if the Church's Creed tells us "we must think thus" of the Trinity, it identifies the correct understanding of the mystery "in opposition to" heretical formulations, such as the Sabellian, Arian and Tri-Theistic positions. None of these deny the Holy Three "in words," though all of them "do deny Him in fact."

Newman closes Volume 6 and concludes *Parochial Sermons* with "Peace in Believing," which positions his readers on the interface between time and eternity. Within time, we are called to faith and endurance in suffering. Yet though time bears upon eternity, it is only one of God's creatures and not everlasting, as Lucretius imagines. The world will end, so will our lives. But in the meantime we prepare for eternity, Newman's ministerial function being to help his audience do that. "For the last six months in our sacred services" he and his readers have traced the history of redemption. All that remains is "to commemorate what will follow at the end," the return of the everlasting reign of God, the infinite peace and blissful perfection [of the Trinity] . . . Now, for twenty-five weeks we represent in figure what is to be hereafter . . . For half a year we stand still, as if occupied solely in adoring Him. 6.369

The doctrine of the Trinity having been for too long "the subject of especial contention" among Christians, Newman's concluding prayer is that the doctrine might be an occasion "not of strife, but of worship . . . not of division, but of unity," a bond of love rather than a basis for enmity.

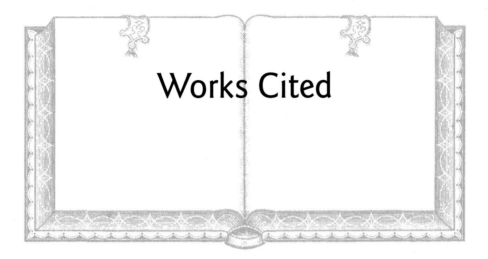

Works Cited

ABRAMS, M. H. *The Mirror and the Lamp: Romantic Theory and the Critical Tradition*. 1953. New York: W. W. Norton, 1958.

———. *Natural Supernaturalism: Tradition and Revolution in Romantic Literature*. New York: W. W. Norton, 1971.

ARISTOTLE. *Rhetoric*. Trans. Roberts. *Great Books of the Western World*, Ed. Hutchins. Vol 9. Chicago & London: Encyclopedia Britannica, 1952.

ARNOLD, Matthew. *The Complete Prose Works of Matthew Arnold*, ed. R. H. Super. Ann Arbor: U Michigan P. Vol 6: *Dissent and Dogma*, 1968. Vol 8: *Essays Religious and Mixed*, 1972.

AUGUSTINE, Saint. *The Confessions of St. Augustine*, Trans. John K. Ryan. New York: Doubleday, 1960.

BLOOM, Harold. *The Visionary Company: A Reading of English Romantic Poetry*. Ithaca and London: Cornell UP, 1971.

CLAY, Diskin. *Lucretius and Epicurus*. Ithaca and London: Cornell UP, 1983.

CHURCH, R. W. *The Oxford Movement: Twelve Years 1833–1845*, 1891. London: Macmillan & Co, 1922.

FAIRCHILD, Hoxie Neale. *Religious Trends in English Poetry*. Vols III and IV, New York: Columbia UP, 1949, 1957; Vols V and VI, New York and London: Columbia UP, 1962, 1968.

HARROLD, Charles F. *John Henry Newman: An Expository and Critical Study*. London, New York, Toronto: Longmans, Green, 1946.

HAVENS, Raymond Dexter. *The Mind of a Poet: A Study of Wordsworth's Thought with Particular Reference to "The Prelude."* Baltimore: Johns Hopkins P, 1941.

HIRSCH, E. D., Jr. "Some Aims of Criticism," 41–62 in *Literary Theory and Structure: Essays in Honor of William K. Wimsatt*, ed. F. Brady, J. Palmer and M. Price. New Haven and London: Yale UP, 1973.

LAMS, Victor J. *Newman's Anglican Georgic*: Parochial Sermons. New York: Peter Lang, 2004.

LUCRETIUS. *The Nature of Things*. Trans. F. O. Copley. New York: Norton, 1977.

NEWMAN, John Henry. *Apologia Pro Vita Sua* (1864). Intro. by A. D. Culler. Boston: Houghton Mifflin, 1956.

———. *Essays Critical and Historical*, Vol I: New York, Bombay: Longmans, Green, 1910.

———. *Essays and Sketches*. ed. With Preface and Introduction by C. F. Harrold. Vol II: New York, London, Toronto: Longmans, Green, 1948.

———. *Parochial and Plain Sermons*. 8 Vols: London, New York and Bombay: Longmans, Green, 1899.

———. *Sermons on Subjects of the Day*. New York & Bombay: Longmans, Green, 1918.

———. "University Preaching" in *Lectures and Essays on University Subjects*. London: Longmans, 1859, 187–220.

ONG, Walter J., S. J. *The Barbarian Within*. New York: Macmillan, 1962, 49–67.

PATTISON, Robert. *The Great Dissent: John Henry Newman and the Liberal Heresy*. New York and Oxford: Oxford UP, 1991.

SEDLEY, David. *Lucretius and the Transformation of Greek Wisdom*. Cambridge: Cambridge UP, 1998.

SHELLEY, Percy. Adonais: *A Critical Edition*. ed. Anthony D. Knerr. New York: Columbia UP, 1984.

SPARK, Muriel. "The Sermons of Newman," *The Critic*, XXII, No. 6 (June-July, 1964), 28–29.

TRACTS FOR THE TIMES, by the Oxford Movement Authors. Vol. I. Oxford: J. Parker, and London: Rivingtons, 1840.

WILLEY, Basil. *The Seventeenth Century Background: Studies in the Thought of the Age in Relation to Poetry and Religion*, 1934. Garden City NY: Doubleday and Co., N. D.

WORDSWORTH, William. *The Fourteen Book* Prelude. ed. W. J. B. Owen. Ithaca and London: Cornell UP, 1985.

Index